Playing for Rangers No. 5

PLAYING FOR RANGERS No. 5

Edited by KEN GALLACHER

STANLEY PAUL, LONDON

STANLEY PAUL & CO LTD
3 Fitzroy Square, London W1

AN IMPRINT OF THE HUTCHINSON GROUP

London Melbourne Sydney Auckland
Wellington Johannesburg Cape Town
and agencies throughout the world

First Published 1973

*This book has been set in Baskerville, printed in Great Britain
by offset litho by Flarepath Printers Ltd., St. Albans, Herts.
and bound by William Brendon of Tiptree, Essex*

ISBN 0 09 117160 1

Contents

One hundred years of greatness

THE three major world club trophies . . . the World Club Championship Trophy . . . The European Cup and the European Cup Winners Cup . . . were paraded around the ground. . . .

The flags of thirty-seven different countries and a host of youngsters wearing the jerseys of the famous clubs from these countries who had met Rangers over the years. . . .

A magnificent match between Rangers, holders of the Cup Winners Cup and World and European champions Ajax of Amsterdam and then to finish everything off a glittering fireworks display.

It was indeed a night to remember. It was a night of soccer pageantry, a night when memories were brought alive and when new memories were made in a fascinating game.

It was the January night that Rangers officially celebrated the opening of their Centenary Year and the ceremony which surrounded that night overshadowed the centenary game a month later which marked the one hundredth birthday of the Scottish Football Association.

Rangers had planned well. The greatest club team in the world was there to mark their 'birthday' and they were there to tell the world that Rangers remained one of the great names in football.

You had only to speak to the greatest of the Ajax stars, Johan Cruyff, the Amsterdam team's captain and striker to realise that. For Cruyff told me: 'We are looking on this as a great honour. Naturally everyone in Europe knows Rangers and for us at Ajax it is a bigger honour to be asked to help them mark their hundred years because we were just a very small club until a few years ago.

'We look on this as an honour to us, too, to be asked to play in Glasgow on such a big occasion. Rangers have always been one of Britain's top teams and that means one of the best teams in Europe and their reputation is formidable.'

8   Rangers' captain John Greig is congratulated by Princess
Alexandra after Scotland's first Royal Cup Final . . . the climax
to Rangers' centenary season!

9

To add to the appeal of the game a huge trophy had been donated by a Dutch newspaper to be played for under the title the 'Super Cup of Europe'. It is still hoped that this Cup will become a regular trophy to be played for by the winners of the two major European tournaments.

Rangers' general manager Willie Waddell who had pulled off the near-impossible task of getting Ajax to cram in two more show games in their hectic schedule, had always been in favour of this idea.

He had agreed to play for the trophy—and though Rangers were banned from Europe there were no objections from the European Union as the game was not officially backed.

But for the two clubs the Cup had an 'official' tag big enough to tempt them to be at their best. . . .

For the clubs the trophy was a very real one, whether it was officially recognised or not. Both clubs saw their clashes as the forerunner of an annual glamour game between the top two teams in Europe.

And for the fans it meant a match with a trophy as well as prestige at stake. Though, of course, with a club as proud as Rangers . . . and a fresher still hungry, club, such as Ajax prestige can so often be enough to bring greatness to any game.

The games were played under European rules—and they are described in the chapter by Derek Johnstone—but it must still be said that fifty-eight thousand fans went to Ibrox on Tuesday, January 16. All of them were there to see the game and also to celebrate Rangers' centenary . . . none of them will forget the night.

It was a soccer extravaganza from the pre-match and after match entertainment to the on-field spectacle so gracefully crowned by the talents of Cruyff.

Afterwards the Dutch skipper insisted: 'We played so well tonight because we knew this was a big occasion. It was more than an ordinary European Cup tie. It was a very special night and all of us in the Ajax side realised that . . . the whole feeling of the stadium brought it home to us so vividly'.

It was that kind of night . . . and it had been necessary for Rangers to have a special, a gala, occasion.

The negotiations had been opened by general manager Willie Waddell six months before in Rotterdam as Ajax clinched their second European Cup win against Inter Milan of Italy. He wanted the best and went after them with the determination that marks his character. He knew that only the BEST would do for this special birthday.

A few months later he was able to announce that he had succeeded in persuading Ajax, who had now added the title of world champions to their formidable honours list.

Little Stefan Kovacs, the Rumanian coach of the Dutch club admitted to me later: 'We have so many games to play that often we cannot answer every request for a match. This time it was different. It was for Rangers and for a very special time in their long and distinguished history and so we decided that we should come to Glasgow.

'Sometimes I am not in favour of extra games because we have such a tough programme. It is enough to tell you that I supported the playing of these matches. . . .'

And, later in the year, it was the same when Arsenal agreed to play the second of the Centenary Celebration games. Other commitments were forgotten . . . because this was Rangers' one hundredth anniversary.

It was, in a sense, almost a fairy tale year for the club. After a disastrous opening to the season they ended their playing year —dating from just before the start of 1973 their special year— by playing twenty-six successive games without defeat. It was the kind of run that revived memories of the great and glorious days of the past . . . the kind of run which will have stories told about it down through the years.

And, strangely, it meant that at the end of the 1972-73 season, just as Rangers slipped into that important '1973' season, their birthday year, they did not lose a single game in competitive football. They lost to Ajax . . . but in the Scottish League and in the Scottish Cup they could not be stopped.

It was as if the gods had decided that in this very special year Rangers must have something very special to celebrate. And that was how it happened. . . .

Because that long unbeaten run was climaxed by their victory over their greatest rivals, the other half of the Old Firm, Celtic, in the Scottish Cup Final. That brought the Cup back to Ibrox after an absence of seven years and rekindled the faith of the fans.

It also meant a fitting finale to the first half of their centenary year . . . a year that will always be remembered.

Which is all that Rangers wanted for their fans . . . good times to remember with affection. The Centenary Year will provide them.

At last the Scottish Cup come back to Ibrox by John Greig

I GAVE up making predictions many, many years ago, mainly because so often I have made them and then lived to regret them. And so before we met Celtic in the Scottish Cup Final last season I made no predictions at all . . . until we were out on the field at Hampden on that May afternoon.

And I know that most of you won't be ready to believe it when I tell you when I made that one and only prediction of last season . . . because I made it just after Celtic had scored the opening goal of the Final.

It probably doesn't seem the right time to any of you for me to suddenly turn and say on the field that we were going to win the Cup . . . but that's when I did it!

For when that Celtic goal went in—a goal scored out of nothing by Kenny Dalglish—I turned to our right back Sandy Jardine and told him: 'Forget that goal . . . because we are going to beat them today. We are going to win that cup. Let's get on with the game and do that. . . .'

And that's the way it worked out for us. There were many reasons for it turning out that way . . . not the least of which was that on the day at Hampden the ball was running for us. That's why I said to Sandy that we were going to win . . . because the little things were going for us.

So often in the past when we have played Celtic on the big occasions things have not run for us. The ball has been bouncing badly, the breaks have gone against us, passes have gone astray. This time—even though Celtic had scored—we were the team who had the ball going our way.

Also, I believe we approached the game with more confidence than we had had for some time before against Celtic. You see we had beaten them in the League at Ibrox at the New Year and since that result we had run them desperately close for their League title, too. We had had a bad start to the season and then suddenly at the end we are right on their heels and we knew that we had worried them.

OK, in the end it didn't come our way in the League and Celtic won it . . . but it was the last day of the season before they could clinch it. And, earlier in the year, it had looked to them and to everyone else that they might have a runaway win with the title.

And, again, we had new players, young players and fresh players who had not known the years of disappointment that I had known myself. The team had been changed a lot and with the change in personnel so had there been a change in attitude. We had young players like Derek Johnstone and Derek Parlane who were desperate to get out there and win medals . . . and new faces like Tom Forsyth and Cutty Young who had that same urge.

Basically the boss, Jock Wallace, had rebuilt and reshaped the team and things had been going so well for us in our League games. We had had our best run for seasons and maybe Celtic were just a bit apprehensive about facing us in that Final. They had had a good run against us in the 'big' ones for so long that maybe they realised that it was coming to an end. Certainly I thought that they came into the game showing a bit of caution in their tactics—showing us more respect than we had been given from them in previous finals.

And their respect was justified . . . because we did win and we did play well and it meant so much to all of us at the Stadium.

At the end of the game the boss, Jock Wallace, was first on that pitch and he came to congratulate me. Afterwards he said that he had done that because of all the disappointments I had had down through the years. He was so right. I had had so many disappointments, so many moments when I felt that we would never win one of the major trophies. So many times when we seemed to be going to win and then finally failed and had the prize taken away from us.

Mind you, this time, though I'd made no predictions until I spoke to Sandy on the field, I hadn't been too worried about the final. The way we were playing I had a feeling that we could win, a feeling that we didn't have to be afraid of anyone after our good League and Cup results.

From the time we beat Hibs in the quarter finals I had the feeling that this could be the year for us. It was another game many people thought we would lose. Hibs were going well, playing with confidence and when they came to Ibrox and gained a draw we were written off. No one could see us going through

This sequence of 12 pictures shows the goal which brought the Scottish Cup back to Ibrox for the first time in seven long years . . . the first goal scored for Rangers by sweeper Tom Forsyth.

14 Derek Johnstone wins this heading duel with George Connelly of Celtic, watched by left to right, Tom Forsyth, Billy McNeil, Dixie Deans, Tom Callaghan and Alfie Conn.

The ball heads for goal . . . and watch Forsyth. As the Celtic   17
defenders hesitate and Derek Johnstone falls, Forsyth is
following up the ball.

18   Alastair Hunter throws himself despairingly to the ball . . .
but it has beaten him . . . and still Forsyth moves in on goal.

Now the ball has hit the post and Forsyth is starting to change direction to get to the new flight of the ball while Hunter lies spreadeagled.

20   As the ball spins tantalisingly along the line suddenly Celtic centre-half Billy McNeil begins his run . . . but he is well away from Forsyth.

to Easter Road and beating Eddie Turnbull's men there when we could not do it at Ibrox, on our own ground.

Yet after that Ibrox draw I felt sure we would win because the Hibs players left after the game celebrating as if they had won. Getting a draw at Ibrox seemed to be all they wanted and so I felt that we could shake them in the replay at Easter Road. We did, too, winning by a goal from Tommy McLean.

That goal, that victory was the confidence booster we needed for the rest of the season, one that helped us beat Hibs in another League game at Ibrox and kept us ready for the final against Celtic.

We prepared so thoroughly for that final, too. Down the week-end previous for a few days at Turnberry Hotel in Ayrshire and then training hard. Then Jock Wallace gave us a thorough tactical rundown on Celtic's style and their players and we were ready. He told each of us the jobs we had to do and what he expected from us and we went onto the field to do what he asked. We won that Cup through a TEAM performance . . . it was a display by a team, by players who wanted to play for each other.

Still, while I say that, I still feel that the younger players deserve a lot of praise. The younger players, and the newer and less experienced Rangers' players, too. Derek Johnstone and Tom Forsyth played magnificently together at the heart of our defence. They picked up the two main Celtic strikers, Kenny Dalglish and Dixie Deans and rarely gave them a kick at the ball. Dalglish scored, and took the ball well, but it had come out of nothing, come at a time when we were making all the running in the game. And the other came from a George Connelly penalty, again at a time when we were on top of the game.

Our goals were better goals, better made goals, better-shaped goals. Derek Parlane took his goal well, so did Alfie Conn and, so, too, did Tom Forsyth though to many people it may have looked a scrambled effort. In the end it was—OK, I accept that. But remember what happened before Tom was there to force the ball over the line at the post. Firstly we had a magnificent header from Derek Johnstone, up in support of the forwards, a header which hit the post. Then, take a look at the pictures here in the book to see how big Tom read the situation from the moment Derek made contact with the ball. He began moving whenever Derek headed the ball and he kept running, not hesitating, not just simply watching the ball, but heading towards goal in case there was a rebound. Other players might not have followed up with the same determination and vision as Tom. But he was there at that post and, though he admits he was so nervous he nearly missed getting the ball over the line, he did it to score his first-ever goal for Rangers. And what an important goal it was for all of us in the team. . . .

It meant an end to seven long, lean and empty years without the Scottish Cup coming to Ibrox and it meant our fans getting the reward they deserved so much for the way they backed us that day. The support at that final was fantastic. I think that lifted us as well on the day. Just knowing all these fans were there to back us meant a lot to the team. It gave us a drive and that joined with the hunger we had for success. One of the Scottish sports writers wrote after the game that we were the hungry team on the day of the Final and that this made the difference between ourselves and Celtic. That probably summed up the game. I think that I agree with that anyhow.

Celtic had won the League just a week before when they beat Hibs at Easter Road and while they had been doing that we had been playing East Fife at Ibrox and winning. But knowing as we did so that Celtic were going to win the League title we had been challenging for.

And so when Hampden came along this was the one chance we had left to WIN something and we all knew that we had to take it.

Then, again, we were slight underdogs—though in an Old Firm game you can never be too much of an underdog—just as Sunderland were underdogs in the English Final. The team who are favourites so often become the team with problems, the team who can be gripped by tension because so much is expected from them.

It's sometimes better to be in there as underdogs, even just the slight underdogs that we were. I think that contributed to the hunger we felt, that hunger I mentioned earlier.

Probably, too, we were helped by the boost we had of going for these two top prizes, the League and the Cup, right to the last moment. We were built up to win one of the honours—and given a bigger boost than ever because we had dragged ourselves into that position after a disastrous start to the season. Perhaps now we may continue to win the trophies at home, perhaps this Scottish Cup win that the players worked so hard to achieve could be the breakthrough we have been needing. I think we might be going to enter the good years again. Of course, I was able to kid some of the other lads in the team as we celebrated the Cup victory at Ibrox after the match . . . kid them because I have four medals and everyone seemed to have forgotten that. I was the only man with a winner's medal in the team which

McNeil and Connelly and Hunter are all desperately trying to reach the ball, but Forsyth is ahead of them, almost on the line and just ready to touch the ball over for the goal that matters so much.

24   Alfie Conn has come into the picture again on the extreme right but Forsyth is the man who matters as he slides the ball over the line at the post.

26   It's over! It's a goal! Forsyth's first goal for Rangers and the
Celtic players are in despair.

Tho momont of joy for Rangers, sadness for Celtic as Forsyth turns away and the ball lies in the corner of the net. It's the goal that has won the Cup.

Celtic skipper Billy McNeil appears to be appealing for offside . . . but as the pictures show the goal was made by Forsyth running from a deep position . . . a position where he was onside.

The anguish of Celtic is shown by Tommy Callaghan on the extreme right of the picture . . . the anger from Billy McNeil as he turns from goal. But the joy belongs to Tom Forsyth and Alfie Conn as they raise their arms in salute.

The fans in the stands go wild as the two Rangers head back to be congratulated by their team-mates. It's the moment Rangers have waited for since last they won the Cup seven years before.

beat Celtic—just demonstrating again the team changes that have been made—and I was captain that last time we won the Cup seven years ago with a Kai Johansen goal.

But I'd won two medals before then and so now I have four altogether—and the youngsters in the team might just be heading into the medal-winning groove too.

Let's face it, we have had lean years—but we have won three major trophies now in three successive seasons!

First of all we won the League Cup . . . then we followed that up with our victory in the European Cup Winners Cup . . . and now we have added the Scottish Cup to make it a hat-trick.

All of these could mean that our big breakthrough for the League is coming. We would love to add that League title to the Cups we have collected. I know that Celtic will play as well as they know how to keep the title they have held for eight years—but we are not going to be overawed by them—because maybe the final showed that they could have more to worry about than we do. We will respect Celtic always—just as they respect us and I know just how closely fought Old Firm games can be. None of these games are easy games . . . all of them are hard, and all of them bring in the fans.

Last season the Final did it again. It was a sell-out—all one hundred and thirty-four thousand tickets sold—and more than one hundred and twenty-two thousand fans were in the ground to see us win. It was the biggest gate in Britain last season, one of the biggest in Europe and it will always remain that. This is one game that just does not lose its magical appeal to the fans. . . .

All I want to do is to keep on the winning side. Our supporters deserve that from us after the bad years.

The World's Greatest Player
by DEREK JOHNSTONE

TWICE last season, twice in the space of two short weeks, I played against the world's greatest footballer. . . .

And, before you begin to go through the contenders for that title in your minds, before you begin to think of all the great players who play so magnificently across the world, let me tell you that, in my opinion, none of them can match the talent and genius of Johan Cruyff.

Cruyff, the slim-line star of Ajax of Amsterdam, the champions of the Netherlands, the champions of Europe, and the champions of world club football, beats them all.

And I feel that I am entitled to give this opinion more than most . . . because I suffered against him!

Sure, I'd known how good he was before Rangers met his team, Ajax, last season. I'd read all about him, watched him often on the telly, and marvelled at some of the goals he had scored. Yet it was only when I had to face him, first at Ibrox and then in the Olympic Stadium in Amsterdam, that I really found out just how great a genius this man is.

He is, of course, the type of player who makes a goal out of nothing. One moment he can be lurking around out on the left hand side of the field—his favourite side—seeming almost disinterested in the game. Then the next moment he is racing in on goal with the ball and scoring.

I don't suppose I'll ever forget the goal he scored against me in the first game at Ibrox. Mind you, he repeated the dose by getting a goal in the second match in Amsterdam, too . . . but it is the first goal that lives with me still.

The games against Ajax had been arranged as the beginning of what might become a regular challenge match, one between the holders of the European Cup and the holders of the European Cup Winners Cup. Last season, of course, the holders were Ajax and ourselves. We were still suffering from a European ban imposed after the troubles in Barcelona but we were allowed to play in friendly games and this was a 'friendly' with a big game tag hung around it from the start. It was the game our general manager Mr. Willie Waddell had wanted. He started negotiations immediately Ajax beat Inter Milan in Rotterdam in the European Cup Final. Later the idea was taken up by a Dutch newspaper and finally the game was clinched.

It was a gala occasion at Ibrox, a tremendous game to mark the club's centenary year. There were fifty eight thousand supporters at the game, all of them looking for something special to make up for the European matches they had been forced to miss in the earlier part of the season.

They saw it, too, even though we were unfortunately on the receiving end. And no one more than me when Cruyff scored the goal of the game just before half time!

I say goal of the game. Looking back now it may very well have been the goal of the season. As I said before, I'll never forget it and these pictures you see here in the book will be on my wall at home to remind me how I was caught out by Cruyff's skills.

In that first game we had decided that I should try to mark him as tightly as possible . . . but it is not an easy job to mark Cruyff, not as easy as it is to mark, say, Gerd Muller of Bayern Munich whom we had faced the year before in Europe.

Muller is more of a static player, dangerous in the box, but outside that eighteen yards' line he cannot cause the same damage as Cruyff. Anyhow, back to THAT GOAL, because it demonstrates so many of his skills.

Firstly it shows his pace. He is as fast as any player I've seen. The fastest man I'd known before was West Brom's Willie Johnston when he was at Ibrox. Maybe over a longish run, fifty yards or so, Willie would win. But from a standing start over that vital first ten or fifteen yards Cruyff is a flier. He would beat anyone, I think.

He started the goal move with that devastating pace and then came his amazing reflexes. And his fantastic instinct. They are what caught me out at the vital moment . . . and made me look like a fool in front of all these fans.

When he went through with the ball, moving clear of me, most players would have shot for goal whenever they got sight of it. Not him. Just as I was trying to get in a tackle—trying in vain I might add—he suddenly pulled on the brakes and I went careering past him. He seemed to be getting ready to shoot and then he changed his mind, stopped, and put his foot on top of

34

the ball to keep it under perfect control. I slithered past him and while I was still trying to make a recovery he had shot for goal. And scored.

He knew he'd scored too. He was turning away from goal with his arm raised in salute before the ball went in. But he knew because he is that type of player. He has this great confidence about him, probably more confidence in his own ability than any other player I've come up against or played with.

And so in that goal we see several of his attributes, his pace and his acceleration, his reflexes—no one else could have stopped the way he did before scoring that goal—and his quickness of thought.

But there are others, as well. His shooting is excellent with both feet—though he favours his left—and he is good in the air. He is also the type of striker who will try for goal whenever he senses an opening.

This is probably why he scores so many spectacular goals. Another contrast with Muller . . . because the little West German doesn't get as many exciting goals as Cruyff does.

The Dutchman, too, is brilliant at making space for himself, even when he is supposed to be tightly marked. Once he drifts away from the man marking him all he has to do is buy himself somehow or other six yards' freedom. If he gets that then most men marking him are dead. That's all the space he needs to get moving, using that tremendously close ball control which he has obviously worked hard to master. He likes to run with the ball, often using diagonal runs across the field, most of them originating from his favourite side, the left. More often than not that's the direction he chooses to drift when he goes out of the middle.

I've covered some of his skills there but his whole greatness as a player is helped by his attitude to the game—both on and off the field. Always he looks upon himself as one of the team. OK, he is the star of the side and he knows that, just as all of us know it. But you won't find him acting that way. He is not a selfish player on the field. If he has a chance to score but then thinks that someone else is better placed to get the goal than he is . . . then the ball is passed to that other player.

We saw him doing that in the games against us, pushing the ball to players who might be in a better position rather than trying for personal glory. He has the same attitude off the field, mixing with the other players just like one of the boys, and apparently he spends a lot of time with the youngsters at the Ajax club. He gets a ball out with the youth team players and

A portrait of Rangers' brilliant young centre half and the player who is already named to become the next Ibrox captain . . . teenager Derek Johnstone.

Opposite, and following pages

This series of photographs shows the goal which Johan Cruyff, the super star of Ajax of Amsterdam, scored against Rangers at Ibrox in the first leg of their European Championship clash. It is the goal which so impressed Derek Johnstone . . . and one of the reasons why Johnstone calls Cruyff the world's greatest player!.

36   Here Johnstone lives through his own agony and Cruyff's ecstasy once more as he provides the words which accompany each of the pictures . . .

'Cruyff is looking up towards me, trying to guage just where I am in relation to him and the goal. I have started to run in an attempt to catch him, but running in such a way as to stay between the ball and the goal. If you look he has already got the ball under control.'

'Now he is making absolutely sure that the ball is completely under control and probably beginning to make up his mind what he is going to do with it. I am still between the ball and the goal, still in the right position.'

37

works with them at the ground . . . probably because he remembers the time when he was just like these youngsters, a schoolboy dreaming about becoming a star. Now he has made it . . . but he hasn't forgotten his beginnings.

For me, that adds to his stature.

We lost the first leg game 3–1 at Ibrox, Cruyff scoring one and making one of the world champions' goals. In the second leg match I wasn't asked to do all the marking. That time we tried to share it between myself and Tom Forsyth, deciding that the man closest to Cruyff should pick him up when they were attacking. It worked a little bettter . . . but again I was the man on the receiving end of a sucker punch when he scored again. We lost 3–2 there and played much better than we had at Ibrox. Alex MacDonald who got our goal in Glasgow did it again in the Olympic Stadium, getting a goal in the first minute.

There were 41,000 fans there and we were twice in front, 1–0 and then 2–1 then they got a soft penalty to make it 2–2 and Cruyff scored the winner.

I was upset about it—I still am any time I think about it now. He had me for a mug twice and, to be honest, I just didn't like it one little bit. I told him so after the game after he had been presented with the giant Cup which had been put up for the match. We were at an after match reception in the stadium when he came across to speak to me and I just told him: 'You've made a fool of me twice with those goals you scored.'

And he answered: 'I was just lucky. These things just come off every so often. They don't always work for me. . . .'

And I said: 'You won't do it a third time against me, anyway. I'll make sure of that!'

Then he grinned and replied: 'We will wait and see. . . .'

Maybe I shouldn't have said it at the reception but I felt so annoyed with myself I had to get it off my chest. Anyway he wasn't worried about it and later on in the evening he told

'This one shows me moving over towards him, getting ready to meet him, because as I am moving so is he. All the time he is edging himself closer towards the Rangers' goal and in a better position to score. I know now I have to close in on him.'

'This is the beginning of the end 'for me. I'm now getting ready to make my tackle . . . while he is starting to drag the ball back with his right foot. It's here that he beat me. I thought he was going to shoot and was still hoping that I would manage to block the shot.'

39

'This is now the vital stage of the whole move. He has made up his mind, come over the ball and then is going to go back to it while I have committed myself to the tackle or the block which I thought was going to be necessary to stop him.'

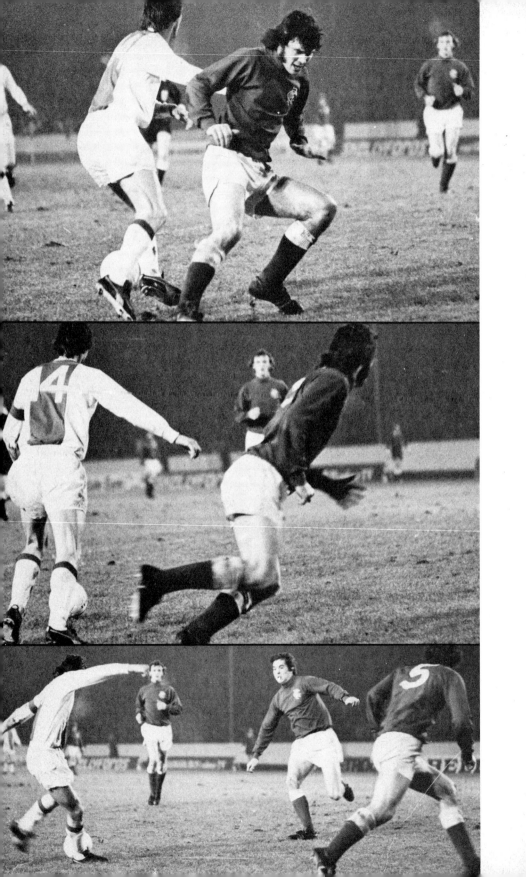

one of the Scottish sports' writers there that he would like to see me in the Ajax team. He thought that I was one of the Rangers' players who would be able to fit into their style. For him to say that about me was a marvellous compliment. I was really pleased when I was told about it afterwards.

After all, Ajax are a superb team. Just as Cruyff is the world's greatest player, they must be rated as the world's greatest club team. And they have a record to prove that . . . being European and world club champions!

They played like world champions too. They are an ambitious team in the football sense, always trying to go forward, always trying to score goals and always trying to entertain while they are winning games convincingly. The defensive strategies which used to strangle soccer at top level, the cattenaccio of the Inter-Milan dominated days, is not for them. They play exciting football, free-flowing football, using a pattern which has every one of their players as a potential attacker. They are geared to that— and able to do it—because all the players in their team are skilful footballers. They have one or two players who can look after themselves physically—but even the 'hard men' can play as well. Their centre half Barry Hulshoff and their West German sweeper Horts Blankenburg and their midfield man Johan Neeskens are no softies. They can be hard when they have to be . . . but they are just as ready to come forward into attack as anyone else when the opportunity to move upfield is there.

This is one of their most impressive features as a team . . . and Cruyff, the captain, plays his role in the general pattern. Often he will drop into a deep position for a spell, taking a breather, I suppose, but covering, too, while others go upfield.

In fact all of the front men have spells like this. They cover for a defender who comes up and then after a little rest they can come back into the game refreshed.

'He's done it now . . . left me stranded. I go slithering past and you can see from the expression on my face that I know now I've been beaten. I look just as sick as I felt at that moment. All I can think of now is getting round and trying to block his shot.'

'I'm wheeling round, trying to get back between him and the goal again but his reflexes are so quick that he has the ball teed up already. He KNOWS exactly what is going to happen now . . . we're still guessing a little.'

'Tom Forsyth is now coming in to help me. He is going to try to block the shot we realise is coming while I make tracks now to get towards the goal line. It's all he has left me . . .'

'This shows just how unlucky Tom was. He was only a split second away from getting a foot in to block the left foot shot. You see him arriving just after the shot has gone for goal.'

'Tom Forsyth is looking towards the goal, so is Willie Mathieson in the background . . . but one man isn't looking at the goal. Cruyff hasn't bothered after he watched his shot go. He knew it was a goal all the way.'

'Cruyff runs back upfield with his arm raised in salute while the realisation that it's a goal hits the Ranger's players, too.'

'It's all over as Cruyff continues his run back to the centre spot to take the congratulations from his mates. It has been the perfectly taken goal.'

All their players seem to have freedom of expression . . . that is, they are allowed to go into any role when a situation demands that. If a gap opens up when a defender has the ball then he can go through that gap . . . or, alternatively, if he doesn't have the ball, he can still make an offensive run to look for it. And while he is out of position then someone else automatically fills in.

We learned a lot from the two games we played against them. We learned how a team should always be ready to play for each other in every sense, in unselfish use of the ball like Cruyff or in readiness to cover for a colleague who is out of position for one reason or another. They all do this in the Ajax side.

We learned, too, that it isn't always the spectacular pass which brings the goals and the victories that you want. For Ajax play the game the easy way . . . proving to me the constant truth of Liverpool manager Bill Shankly's view that football is 'a simple game'. Ajax have players who play the easy ball all the time and the easy ball the way they use it is the one that provides difficulties for whichever team is playing against them.

I learned, too, that if I am ever asked to play against Cruyff again at any other time in the future then I'll try to get to him quickly as he gathers a ball. The one way you seem able to upset him is by biting into tackles early . . . going in hard just as he tries to bring the ball under control. That's the one chance you have of getting on top of him. Because if you let him get the ball under control and then let him start moving towards you then you've had it. But if he has a weakness then it is that he does not relish hard tackles. I'm not suggesting that I'd foul him, or play dirty. But I would play him hard in a bid to upset him.

He reacts badly to hard tackles now, possibly because he has had to take a lot of rough treatment in his time. Certainly it cannot be that he isn't used to tackles because Dutch football is much the same as our own in terms of physical contact.

I hope I do get another chance to renew my personal duel with Cruyff and to play against Ajax. I know how much our fans enjoyed the two games—and we took a big support to Amsterdam with us for the second leg even though the European Union considered it a 'friendly'.

They had to say that because of the year long ban we had received. But for that it would have been recognised as a challenge game between the holders of Europe's top two trophies.

I know that's how we looked on it, and how the fans looked on it, and how the Ajax players looked on it too. We had too much prestige at stake to consider it as a mere 'friendly' and I think Ajax were the same. They didn't want their reputation dented by losing to us.

At Ibrox they caught us a little by surprise and that's why we lost so decisively there—though the game moved our way after half time. But that was too late to save the first leg. . . .

It was different in Amsterdam and but for a daft penalty decision we might have drawn with them. We might even have won!

As it was we lost by one goal but we scored twice . . . the first

44

foreign team to do that against Ajax in their own stadium for nearly ten years. Our performance was a bit of a boost for us and the standard we reached that night was underlined just a couple of months later when our old European foes, Bayern Munich, the West German champions, went to the same ground in the quarter final of the European Cup.

The game was hailed everywhere as 'the final before the final' and certainly it was the game that Cruyff and Co. had wanted to reserve for the final. But all the glory expected from the two teams came from just one of them that night in Amsterdam . . . it came from Ajax who scored four goals!

They beat Bayern 4–0 and that humiliation of the West German cracks, Franz Beckenbauer, Gerd Muller and all the rest, proved to me just how well we had played there.

The two games we had against Ajax were among the highlights of a season which had seemed drab to begin with because of that Europe ban hanging around our necks, but which eventually sparkled for Rangers as a team and for me personally.

You see it was also the season I was asked to captain Rangers when the regular skipper John Greig was injured. I didn't expect that honour but team boss Jock Wallace handed the ball to me before the League Cup semi-final replay at Hampden against Hibs.

I thought the honour would have gone to one of the more experienced players but I enjoyed it. It carries a bit of responsibility on the field but the other lads were ready to help me. Now the Boss has said I'll be the next captain of Rangers when Greigy decides to retire and I know just how much of an honour that is. It's something that schoolboys all over Scotland dream about and here am I going to get it.

It means a lot but as long as I have these pictures of Cruyff's Ibrox goal to jog my memory then there's no danger of getting carried away with the honour.

Just looking at them will bring me back to earth any time. . . .

A Conversation with the 'New Boys'

Quinton Young and Tom Forsyth were the first team 'new boys' for Rangers last season. Outside left Young, known as Cutty to his Ibrox team-mates, came from Coventry City as part of the transfer deal which took centre forward Colin Stein south to the English First Division club. Teak-hard sweeper Forsyth moved from Motherwell to Rangers in a £40,000 transfer deal around the same time.

Both players became vital parts of team boss Jock Wallace's re-building programme. Both arrived at a bad stage in the season, at a time when Rangers were struggling to find the form which later came easily to them . . . but both wanted desperately to play for Rangers and to help them back to greatness.

The following conversation came about after I had decided to ask these two fresh faces in the first team pool just what differences they had known playing for Rangers as opposed to playing for their other—lesser-known—clubs.

Gallacher: Tom, you spent a longish time with just the one senior club, Motherwell, while Cutty had a spell with Ayr United and then some time in the south with Coventry. What makes it different now being with Rangers?

Forsyth: Well, straight away the first thing that gets to you is that every week, no matter which team you are playing nor where the game is, you are going out on that field to win. There is never any thought about playing for a draw or anything like that. You have to get out there and win and luckily most weeks after I first joined up at Ibrox we were doing that.

Young: That's just how I felt, too . . . to be going for victory all the time is a change. Let's face it when I was at Ayr we quite honestly went to some games expecting to be hammered. It's different here at Ibrox. We go to win and when we're doing it then no place on earth is better football-wise.

46

Forsyth: Cutty talks about Ayr and it was the same at
Motherwell. You hoped for the best in some of the games against
the top clubs but deep down you felt that in these games you
were going to lose. Like, when you played Rangers and Celtic,
then you raised your game, played out of your skin, really, but
you didn't beat them very often.

Young: If you did beat them it was just the greatest thing
that could happen to you. Of course Ayr were part-time and
I was still working down the pits and it was something really
special to win against the Old Firm. I remember beating Rangers

Tom Forsyth, who became the anchor man of the Ibrox   47
defence, mops up an opposition attack watched by two of
his team mates Derek Johnstone, and Dave Smith.

once at Somerset Park and the champagne was out in the dressing room . . . and that was just for winning a League game. It only meant two points, nothing else.

Even at Coventry we weren't expected to win when we went away from home. You went to away games looking for a draw.

You know how it is, down in England a point away from home is a bit of an achievement. Consequently you dropped into a defensive formation when you left your own ground. You went to matches with a negative outlook . . . here it's so different. I can honestly say that there wasn't a game last season

48   Cutty Young sends in a shot for goal . . . and it was this kind of determination and goal-hunger which brought him the backing from the fans that he knew he needed.

whether it was at Dens Park or Easter Road or anywhere else that Rangers had instructions to play for a draw. It's not tolerated. We are expected to go out and win. I like it . . . and I like winning, too.

Gallacher: Do you think this business of winning most of your games builds confidence?

Young: I think it does. I'd never really known it before because at Ayr and Coventry you spent most of your time fighting for survival, looking over your shoulders in case you slipped too close to relegation. Now, with Rangers, you talk about titles and winning Cups and getting into Europe. It's a completely different life.

Forsyth: Winning helps and the whole attitude around the club helps and the fans help, too. When you are with a provincial club—and I had five years with one at Motherwell—you get to the stage that you're going to grounds for games and you know that there won't be any atmosphere. It was like playing on ghost grounds, at times. There were so few fans coming to the games that the atmosphere was just dreadful and that affects players. You find it hard to raise your game in that type of situation.

That all changes when you are with the Rangers. You go to places like Arbroath and find something like fifteen thousand fans behind you. It's something you never knew before and it helps your game. At least I think it has helped me. You thrive on big match atmosphere, any player will tell you that.

Young: That's perfectly true. When you are with a small club in Scotland you don't get the chance, too often, to experience that atmosphere, a real big match feeling. Really you get it four times a year . . . in your games against the Old Firm.

Gallacher: Although Rangers were banned from Europe last year the pair of you still managed to get a taste of what European football is all about, and what Europe means to Rangers and their fans, when you played Ajax. How did you feel about that one?

Young: It was tremendous. Just to be on the same field as some of these Ajax players meant a lot to me. I'd played against a few foreign teams when I was with Coventry. One close season we toured a bit and played Olympiakos of Greece and the Korean national side and we also met Santos who were in the Far East at the same time as we were. The Brazilians, Pele and the rest, were the best team I'd come up against until Rangers played Ajax. Honestly Ajax would have beaten Santos easily.

Forsyth: I'd played for Scotland in an international in

Denmark one summer and I'd been to Italy with Motherwell . . . but that was the lot as far as foreign opposition was concerned. And the Motherwell thing wasn't much.

We went to Italy and finished up playing some unknown team. It's not like going somewhere with Rangers and facing the Milans or Inter-Milans or Torinos or any of the big names. Motherwell just didn't get that kind of chance.

The Ajax game was great . . . it was starting out at the top so far as I was concerned. Two or three months before that match I was just playing away quietly at Motherwell knowing the best chance of coming up against teams from outside Scotland was a place in the Texaco Cup. Then, BANG, I'm playing against the European Cup holders and guys like Cruyff. That showed me right away just what it's all about in Europe. I could hardly wait after that for the chance to get into the European tournaments.

Gallacher: We started off talking about differences in playing for Rangers as compared with other clubs and we've covered some changes in your careers. But how about off-field changes? Tom, you must know a difference, especially, with only being at Motherwell before. With Cutty having a spell at Coventry maybe it won't be all new to him.

Forsyth: It's like night and day so far as the facilities offered to the lads are concerned. I know that some of the boys probably don't think anything about it because they have always been at Ibrox and are used to the set-up. But for anyone coming from a smaller club it's fantastic.

There's the indoor track for working out any time you want to. You can do weight training and circuits in there and there's the sauna bath to keep you toned up, and you get regular massage and medical checks. The medicals come every three months and these are really thorough. The doctor comes in and gives you a right going over. We didn't have that kind of treatment at Motherwell. Sauna baths and the like are luxuries for me. . . .

Young: I know what Tom means because I felt the same about things when I went south to Coventry first of all. But, as you say, having been in England, I'm more used to it now. But, believe me, I knew that this set-up would be first class otherwise I wouldn't have come back to Scotland. I enjoyed it in the south and there were a few clubs interested in me. Hull and Cardiff and Notts Forest all wanted to buy me when Coventry decided to sell and at the start I hadn't even thought about coming back home. And I wouldn't have come back for

50

any other club except Rangers. That's the truth!

Gallacher: Was that just because you knew the set-up was so professional, as good as any in England, or simply because Rangers were the club you wanted to play for.

Young: A bit of both, I suppose. I did want to play for Rangers—I always had because they were the team I used to support as a kid. When I went to Ayr from the juniors I heard a lot of rumours about how Rangers were interested in me. I kept hoping they would come after me but nothing happened.

All the lads at Somerset knew I was Rangers daft and they used to kid me about it. This chance to come to them when I moved from Coventry came out of the blue. But when I was told it was Rangers then that was it—I knew I was coming home.

Gallacher: How about you, Tom, were you the same?

Forsyth: More or less. I came from Stonehouse in Lanarkshire —and I still stay out there—so as a boy I supported two teams, Motherwell and Rangers. Motherwell because they were close to me and I could go to watch their games and Rangers, well, because they were the team I would really have liked to go and see every week. Any time I was at a Motherwell game the first result I was looking for when I got home was the Rangers result. Like Cutty I didn't think twice when I was told that Rangers wanted me. It was my ambition to play for them.

Gallacher: Now that you are there, that you've achieved ambitions, do you feel there are more pressures on your game?

Forsyth: Naturally there are . . . because you are always expected to be winning games. If you lose a match it's like a national disaster. And you have to remember that every other team is out to beat Rangers. I know that because we were that way at Motherwell. We used to play our guts out against Rangers —you see there was atmosphere for these games and the players responded. They rose to the occasion and so do the teams, which makes it harder again.

Young: It gets back to this thing that you are expected to win all the time, week after week, game after game. But I'll settle for that kind of pressure rather than the pressure that comes from fighting off relegation. I like winning. I enjoy it . . . because I've never known it happen to me so regularly than since I joined the Rangers.

Gallacher: One for you, Cutty. You were away for a couple of seasons in England. When you came back to play up here which teams impressed you more than before you left Ayr and which Ibrox players impress you now that you are playing alongside them?

Young: Well, I suppose there are still some teams who haven't improved any but Hibs, Aberdeen and the two Dundee sides, Dundee and United, have played well against us. United are very well organised.

The real change coming home is to find that the game up here is now more physical than it is in England. It used to be the other way about but since the referee clampdown in England things are better there. Tackling from behind is stopped . . . but in Scotland it still goes on. If you don't believe me then you can take a look at the backs of my legs sometimes.

In the Rangers team I've been impressed by the two youngsters Derek Parlane and Derek Johnstone. Derek Parlane wasn't in the team when I went south and he has done really well. Derek Johnstone was in the team but was a sixteen years old centre-forward then . . .now he is a centre-half. And what a centre-half!

In two years' time he will be the best centre-half in Britain. Just watch him. He has so much skill for a defender.

And then there's Willie Mathieson, a player few people ever mention, but now that I'm playing down that left side in front of him I know just how much work he does for the team.

Gallacher: Tom, how about you and your new team? How do you feel about the role you have and the way things have gone for you?

Forsyth: Well, I had the worst kind of start, getting injured and being off for a month or so not long after I signed. But I think I got over that OK. I worried about it at the time. You know how it is when you join a new club and you are dying to establish yourself . . . then you are injured. It's a terrible feeling.

Still, that's past me. I love it now and I enjoy playing 'sweeper'. It's my favourite position and playing beside Derek Johnstone is good for anyone.

I have had a lot of encouragement from the fans, too. They help you. It's funny thinking back to the Motherwell days now. Before I signed for Rangers I could have walked through Glasgow unrecognised. I could have strolled up and down Argyll Street or Sauchiehall Street all day and no one would have known me. Now that's impossible and there are so many supporters' club functions to go to . . . it's great. I enjoy that.

Gallacher: Finally, what ambitions do you have left in the game now?

Forsyth: I just want to help Rangers win as many honours as possible, and stay in the first team while they're winning them. That includes in Europe. I'd like to help them win another trophy there, too.

Cutty Young gives the effort demanded from Rangers in their training sessions as he powers into this sprint at the Albion Training ground.

53

Young: Tom's said just about it all. I want the same and I want it as much for the fans as for ourselves.

I have a lot to be grateful to them for. I came to Ibrox just as Colin Stein was going and I knew he'd been a big favourite with the fans. Because of that I had a few worrying moments, just wondering how they would take to·me. There wasn't any need for the worry. They were great. If they hadn't been so good to me at the beginning then I might have struggled a bit. They helped me to settle down and I'll never forget that.

Forsyth: The same goes for me. Having them on your side makes all the difference. . . .

54   This is the luxury life that Tom Forsyth now enjoys . . . the sauna bath style that makes Ibrox so different from his days with Motherwell at Fir Park.

There had to be some changes made

by JOCK WALLACE

WHEN I took over as team manager of Rangers, when Willie Waddell stepped aside after the European Cup Winners Cup victory in Barcelona, and gave me my chance to handle the team on my own, I knew that there would have to be changes made. . . .

I suppose most people look at a team which has been outstandingly successful and immediately reckon that this is the best time for a new manager to take over. Somehow, though, it doesn't work out that way. Success can provide the new manager with headaches . . . just as failure can. Success, in fact, can prove an obstacle to a new manager.

That was the way I felt about it last year. There I was taking over a team which had just won the first European trophy in the near-hundred-year history of Rangers. Many great Rangers' teams in the past had tried to do that. Teams which had had more success at home in Scotland had tried to do that . . . and all of them had failed. All of them, that is, until the team I had worked with as a coach under Willie Waddell's managership beat the Russian side Moscow Dynamo in that Barcelona final.

That one victory had put these players among the Ibrox immortals. They deserved to be there, too and they also deserved all the praise that was showered on them through that momentous European run. I didn't grudge them one bit of that.

They had earned it all with a succession of magnificent matches in Europe. They deserved all of it after their display of courage in Lisbon, of discipline in Turin and of skill in Munich. And no one could deny that they had indeed become 'immortal' because of their European success.

But that very fact was what worried me. I knew that having a team of players who were being told constantly that they were 'immortal' wasn't going to be of much use to me. I didn't want a team lying back resting on its laurels after a great success. I

55

wanted a team which was still hungry, still looking for more success in the season ahead.

I had to make sure that the players would remain hungry and to do that I knew that I would have to 'stir the pot'. I had to have them thinking hard about their roles in the team, about their first team positions. I had to have them on edge and I could do that by showing them that the team could do without them. The successes in Europe had come from team work and a great team spirit which had grown up amongst the lads and I had to keep that going too. I knew that this was going to prove the difficulty for me. Because I had to preserve that high spirit and make my changes at the same time.

I worried about that at the start of last season. I had ideas in my mind about what I wanted to do. But, I also knew, that after winning a European trophy you cannot begin immediately by making changes. There has to be a time, a right time, to make the changes you want to make and to start re-building the team the way you want to do it.

Basically my problems centred round two of the players, centre forward Colin Stein and outside left Willie Johnston and these were the players who had scored our goals in Barcelona! Steiny had got one of them and the other two had been scored by Bud (Johnston's nickname among the Rangers' players—editor). Now, though, in spite of these goals I felt that we had to have them out of the team before getting the rhythm going the way I wanted it to go.

Two goal hero Willie Johnston holds the European Cup Winners Cup in the Barcelona dressing room. But a few months later he was transferred . . . one of the stars who had to leave Rangers, says manager Jock Wallace.

Don't get me wrong on this. It was not a personal matter. I have nothing against the two players . . . it was simply a question of how I wanted to run the team. There just had to be some changes and these two players were eventually sold, Stein to Coventry and Johnston to West Bromwich Albion. They didn't go because I discounted their ability . . . but because they were two players who wanted to do things in their own way. That was something I couldn't afford to have.

It was obvious to me that I was not going to get either of them to do things MY way. And if they weren't going to follow instructions then we had to get players who would.

Any manager MUST have things done his way. There cannot really be any other method in 'bossing' a team. No compromises, no one influencing your decisions . . . just a straight-ahead attitude of getting on with the job the way that you want to get on with it. Sometimes that can make you unpopular but, again, that shouldn't affect you or influence you in any way at all.

Once I'd made up my mind on the changes I wanted—and that came after one or two damaging results early in the season —then I discussed the whole situation with Willie Waddell. I told him what I intended to do and he immediately backed me all the way.

I'd like to make it clear here just how much I owe to Willie Waddell. He has given me my chance as team manager, as well as bringing me to Ibrox in the first place, and, though he was team boss before me, he has never interfered with any decisions

Team boss Jock Wallace emphasises a point with a clenched fist in the dug out as he watches his team along with Rangers' physiotherapist Tom Craig.

I have made. Anything connected with the playing side of the game is my area of control and none of my decisions in that area is altered. I can ask advice—and I do it because I know that the advice I get from him will be good advice. And we can have arguments, but not serious arguments which cause a rift between us . . . it's the kind of argument we both find stimulating.

Anyhow, as I said, he gave me his full support for my plans to re-shape the side, saying to me 'What's taken you so long?'

I knew, of course, I had delayed a little but then one or two bad results made it easier for me to make the changes I had been contemplating.

58   Tommy McLean shows the kind of ball control that Jock Wallace knew he could not improve on . . .

Here is the new side to maestro McLean as he challenges for the ball the way Wallace wants him to do.

Colin Stein was transferred first, because he wanted to play one way while I wanted him to play another. So he went to Coventry City and Quinton Young arrived at Ibrox along with a sizcable fee in our favour.

Then Willie Johnston moved, partly, again, because he was so individualistic and also because he had his problems with the SFA Referee Committee.

These are the two players who left the club and so I had the job, then, of filling their positions and getting on with the other changes I had in mind.

We had Quinton Young as a natural left wing replacement for Willie Johnston. He arrived at Ibrox and straight away proceeded to do a tremendous job for us. In fact, before the end of the season, he had become one of the highest scoring wingers in the country after spending only two thirds of the season with us. His record speaks for itself. . . .

Then it was a replacement for Stein we wanted and, while some of the fans probably don't realise it even yet, I knew from the start that the man to take his place as centre-forward, was already on the staff . . . Derek Parlane.

I did try to buy another centre-forward, Kenny Mackie from Dunfermline, but the idea there was to have Mackie teaming up with Parlane in a twin striker set-up. There was never any doubt in my mind that Parlane was going to take over from Stein.

Originally the thought was for Mackie to play up front with Parlane dropping slightly deeper and I'm sure it would have been successful. I shook up a few fans by offering big money for Mackie, a Second Division teenager few people had heard of.

But, before the end of the season—after he had refused to come to Ibrox—English clubs were forming long queues outside East End Park as they tried to sign him.

I took that as a compliment to our Ibrox scouting system . . . because we moved for the kid long before anyone else came along!

Still, when Mackie didn't come Derek was left to go it alone in the main striker's role and he relished both the role and the responsibility which went with it. I had always known he would come through into the first team and I always felt that he would come through as a striker, even though it was his appearance in midfield against Bayern Munich at Ibrox the previous season which blasted him into the first team pool. He has worked hard and listened well and last season he came on even faster than I had anticipated. Inside a few months the boy blossomed into one of the country's best strikers and I had honestly expected it to take a little longer before he struck that kind of form for us.

After these changes it was Rangers' turn to move into the transfer market and the money we had from our sales was partially spent on two players, veteran forward Joe Mason from Morton and our defensive anchor man Tom Forsyth from Motherwell.

Now Joe Mason is just the kind of lad managers like to have around a club, eager to learn, always proud to be with a top team after so many years with lesser outfits, and someone who is ready to pass on his experience to the younger players. He didn't make a whole lot of first team appearances but he helped us during a sticky spell and he was a handy man to have around in the pool of players. As well as being a good dressing room influence!

Here is a sequence of four pictures demonstrating the ability and courage of goalkeeper Peter McCloy . . . a man named as 'another Yashin' by team boss Wallace.

McCloy has left his line and is launching himself forward onto the ball as Morton forward Donnie Gillies races to meet it on the six yards' line.

McCloy has won the race, gathering the ball safely and tucking down his head as Gillies clashes with him.

Gillies takes off, flying over McCloy's body as the giant 'keeper hugs the ball to his chest.

Tom Forsyth stands guard now as McCloy prepares to rise and Gillies slumps on the ground. It has been the perfectly timed, perfectly read save, just one of many McCloy made last season for Rangers.

Tom Forsyth was someone I had always admired when he was with Motherwell. I had wanted him in the side and so we moved in to buy him. He is big and strong and determined and he desperately wanted to play for the Rangers. He developed so well for us, reading the game well from his 'sweeper's' position and forming a fine partnership at the centre of the defence with young Derek Johnstone. He tackles like a tank and so he brought iron into our defence.

These were the changes made in personnel . . . but there were other changes, too. Changes in approach for instance. Take wee Tommy McLean as an example. I knew, like everyone else, where Tommy's strengths lay and I knew, too, that there was no one in the world who could tell the wee man how he could improve on his passing or on his striking of a ball. I certainly wasn't going to try it and so we worked away at other aspects of his game that needed tightening up. He had his natural gifts that we could improve on . . . so we had to add another dimension to his game. That's why I began asking him to chase back more than he had ever done in the past, asking him to harry his opposing full-back whenever the back was in possession of the ball. I had to get it through to him that when he lost the ball he had to fight to try to get it back. Or, if he couldn't get it back, make sure that the man who had taken the ball from him wasn't going to threaten us unopposed. Last season he was doing all of these things just the way we wanted him to do them.

It wasn't something that came naturally to him. But I felt that we had to instil this into his game and, though I know that this was something else which brought me criticism, I know, too, that it worked. Tommy began to chase back and help out the defence when we needed him to do that and he still had these matchless talents of his for striking the ball and passing and crossing unimpaired. We had added to his game and he had one of his best-ever seasons for Rangers . . . that answers any criticism. And it also proves my point that a change in a player's approach can work wonders.

We work on all the players and sometimes we see more from some in a season than from others. Last season we were lucky in seeing a lot of the training ground work paying off . . . and one of the happiest pay offs for me was in the form shown by Peter McCloy in goal. I spent a lot of time with Peter and he responded to the coaching he received. Last season he was the best goalkeeper in Britain in my opinion and I can honestly see him develop into another Lev Yashin. He has everything and in comparing him to the great Russian goalkeeper I can't praise him any higher.

Then there's Willie Mathieson, one of the unsung heroes of the team. No one knows he is there . . . except the other players and myself! We know his value to the team only too well because he is one of the most dependable players at Ibrox. He spent a long time at Ibrox before eventually breaking through into the first team.

It had been a bit of a struggle for him, I suppose, and he doesn't forget that. So he still has this hunger for success about him and he works so very hard. He is sometimes sold short by the fans . . . but the players know just how valuable Willie is to us.

And then there's John Greig who has done it all. He's won every honour, captained Rangers and Scotland, and yet stays as enthusiastic as a youngster just coming into the game. He is the inspiration of the team, a tremendous influence both on and off the field and the perfect captain. He is a man you can always rely on . . . and even now at his stage in his career you still find him working to improve his game. What more can you ask for?

The lads are all that way. I know what I want from them and they know it too and accept it. I think that they realise there is a way to go before I have the team that I want at Ibrox . . . and they had that brought home to them when we played Ajax of Amsterdam last season in a two-leg challenge game. They are the ideal team in my book. They have skill and speed and strength in all the right places . . . and they have quite magnificent on-field organisation. I have been tremendously impressed by them and their performance against the West German cracks Bayern Munich in the first leg of the European Cup quarter final in Amsterdam last season was perfection. They are the team I would like to model Rangers after. . . .

It was a tremendous experience for us to play against them twice last season. The players had missed Europe and all the opportunities and excitement that playing in one of the top Continental tournaments throw up for club and players. Having to face up to a team of the quality of Ajax demonstrated to them more forcefully than I could have told them just what we are after, what we are aiming to achieve at Ibrox. We had a good end to the season when we pushed the players hard and we got the response we looked for from them—in some cases we got more than we looked for—and I think that the Ajax game coming when it did helped us.

OK, I know that we didn't beat them. I know that we lost twice . . . but we came out of the two games with a lot of credit.

I don't mind admitting that I was angry after the first game at Ibrox . . . not at my players because we lost but because everyone kept talking about what Ajax had done and ignored anything that we had done. They forgot how well we had played in the second half of that game at Ibrox . . . and so, in Amsterdam, I was delighted that we maintained that second half form for the whole ninety minutes. We lost 3–2 but our result was one of the best achieved by a foreign team playing against Ajax in Amsterdam during the years they have played in European football. We showed then just how well we could play but basically, we learned just how much we still have to do to become a great team. Ajax are the top . . . and we have them to aim at.

I want Rangers to be the top team in Scotland—and I know that's what Rangers want more than anything else, but then Rangers have been part of my life too, even before I joined the club as coach. Way back as a youngster I used to come through from my home in the east of Scotland and stand on the terracings with the other members of the local supporters' club.

That's why I want to help them be the top team . . . because it's the position they should always be in.

Here is Rangers' left back Willie Mathieson watching a shot being blocked by a former Old Firm Rival, ex-celt John Clark now with Morton. Mathieson is too often overlooked says boss Wallace.

The 'Tiger' picks his All-Time Greats

JOCK SHAW—or 'Tiger' Shaw as he was to so many thousands of Rangers' fans in the glory days just after the war—was captain of the Ibrox club for sixteen successful seasons. His reign as skipper lasted from 1938 until he retired from football in 1954.

He was club captain at a time when the Rangers' teams were packed with fiercely individual players, and with some of the greatest stars that Ibrox has ever known. Before he joined Rangers to become their captain in 1938 Shaw had been Airdrie's left-back for five years. But always, at heart, he had been a Rangers' man. Now fifty-nine years old Shaw keeps his connection with the club, working as a member of the ground staff and keeping his memories of Rangers alive. These memories stretch back for half of the hundred years the club has been in existence. He remembers watching Rangers as a boy, as a young man, and then playing against them in his seasons with Airdrie as well as during that long, long spell of captaincy.

From all these viewpoints, from all these memories of players down the years, memories forged out of playing alongside them or simply watching them, Jock Shaw has picked the team he feels would be the finest-ever side to come out of Ibrox.

He says: 'I've tried to pick a team with several ideas in mind . . . ability, determination, skill and loyalty to Rangers. I suppose, really, I've based my choice, a completely personal choice, on men I enjoyed playing with and others I know I would have enjoyed playing with.

'There have been so many great players over the years that it has not been easy. It's never easy to do this and I know that my choice won't be the same as others would make. But this is the team I would have loved to play in. This is the team I honestly think would have been the best Rangers' team ever. . . .'

And so here it is . . . 'Tiger's' team, a parade of greats stretching down through the years and across the generations.

Goalkeeper—Jerry Dawson—'They called Jerry the "Prince of Goalkeepers" in Scotland and I would go along with that. I can't go past him when I'm asked to name a team. He was the complete goalkeeper and a fantastic personality as well. When I played in front of him he always had a tremendous understanding with myself and the right-back Dougie Gray. We knew when Jerry was going to come off his line, we didn't have mixups about that. He was superb at cutting out crosses and his judgment was perfect. He was agile and he was intelligent and he could read the game from his line. Some of the saves he made were uncanny. He was one of the finest goalkeepers I have ever seen.

'Now, perhaps over the past season Peter McCloy has shown signs of emerging as another Dawson. The signs are there in the way he wants to COMMAND his area . . . which is what Jerry did all the time.'

Right-back—Dougie Gray—'He was my full-back partner when I first went to Ibrox and there was a great thing about Dougie which would always carry him into any Rangers' team I could pick. He had—allied to his ability—a tremendous feeling for the club.

'Dougie loved the Rangers. He was only happy when we had won. If we lost then Dougie was miserable. He would have done anything to help Rangers win and be successful. He was a great club man. He was a good tackler, two footed and tremendously fast in recovery. He didn't win caps because there were a whole lot of good full backs around then . . . people like Jimmy Carabine and others. But for Rangers he was a wonderful player.'

Left-back—Sammy Cox—'Sammy played for a long, long time in front of me as a left-half and then when I went out of the team he stepped back to take my place. He became the complete full-back and easily the most deadly tackler I ever saw. He wasn't powerfully built or anything, but his timing in the tackle was perfect. He was one of the few full-backs who could handle Stanley Matthews or Tom Finney when he was playing for Scotland and they were in the Eglish team. But it wasn't only his defensive qualities that made Sammy stand out . . . he was a brilliantly constructive player as well. Maybe it was his years as a left-half which gave him this because he could use the ball superbly. And, in his day, remember, that was not expected from a full-back!'

Goalkeeper Peter McCloy . . . last season, says Tiger Shaw,   67
the Ibrox 'keeper approached the greatness of the legendary
Jerry Dawson.

68   Rangers' general manager Willie Waddell who has brought all the determination he showed as a player to the job of bossing Rangers back to glory.

Right-half—Ian McColl—'He impressed me in his days at Ibrox because he was so determined to become a good player. He worked and worked at his game and when he knew that his passing was letting him down a little then he would be spending time on that aspect of his game until it reached the standard he wanted. He could always bring a ball down magnificently and he was a solid player, a team player, who would help out any of his team-mates if they were in trouble. He was, in fact, the type of player that every team needs. Dependable. Reliable. Honest.'

Centre-half—Willie Woodburn—'There can be only one choice here . . . and that's Woodburn. He was the ideal centre-half, the complete centre-half, if you like. I just can't say enough about him as a player. He was two footed, strong in the tackle, and just about unbeatable in the air. Then add to that the fact that he possessed so much more skill than the ordinary run of centre-halves at that time—or even today!

'The laddie we have now, Derek Johnstone, is the only player I've seen to come even close to Woodburn as far as skill goes. He could be as good and if he does make it then he'll be the best centre-half in the world. Because that's what Woodburn was.

'His one weakness was himself. He has this quick temper which would land him in trouble on the field. But when you see what is allowed to go on nowadays on the field you wonder if he was as bad as people believed at the time. Willie Woodburn was given a *sine die* suspension but there are players playing today who have behaved far worse than he ever did.'

Left-half—Jim Baxter—'Again there can be no argument about this choice. Like Woodburn there is just no way that you can go past Baxter for any team of Ibrox greats. He was the most wonderful, the most talented left-half I've ever seen. When he was here at Ibrox and playing at his peak then he was world class. During that spell he had with Rangers in the 'sixties Baxter had so much talent that he would have walked into any of the world's top teams. That's how good he was. His passing was deadly accurate, his ball control was unbelievable and his left foot was magical. That left foot was better than any other left foot I've ever seen. You just can't ignore Baxter because he had so much talent and because he had a tremendous impact on Rangers at that time.'

Outside-right—Willie Waddell—'Like Woodburn and Baxter

70   Derek Johnstone—one of the present-day squad who so
very nearly forced his way into the all-star team chosen by
former Rangers' captain Jock Shaw.

. . . Waddell was unique. There was only one Willie Waddell. He had tremendous strength and running power and could hit the ball with either foot. It didn't seem to matter to him which foot the ball went to. He was a natural.

'He was the type of player who could transform a whole game for you. I mean, we could be back on our heels in a match, defending desperately and then the ball would be played out to Waddell and he'd be off, making for the opposition goal. Like as not he'd finish up scoring. He had this flair for turning a game. I couldn't begin to count the number of times he has done that for us. He had tremendous determination, too. The same determination that he has brought to the manager's job . . . a determination to help Rangers succeed. When I look at him from a left-back's point of view then I can remember just how hard a man he was for anyone to face. He had a way of cutting in and then letting loose a shot for goal that made him one of the most dangerous wingers football has ever seen.'

Inside-right—Torry Gillick—'If you have Waddell in the team then you simply have to have Gillick. The two go together, they were a partnership, and the best right-wing partnership that Rangers ever had! Gillick had a tremendous vision about him in the game. To me he was like a billiards' player, always making a move in a game with the next move in mind. I think that's honestly the best way I can describe him. Billiards' players always play for the next shot, always size things up in advance . . . and Torry was the same on the football field.

'It was uncanny the way that Torry seemed to know how the game was going to progress. He had this vision for the game, almost a sixth sense for soccer, and I didn't know anyone else who had it. And he was perfect in partnership with Waddell. The two of them complemented each other perfectly.

'The one player who would challenge Torry's position would be Ian McMillan who was so richly talented and who did so much in his time with Rangers. But it's a team I'm picking and where Waddell is outside right then Gillick is his partner.'

Centre-forward—Willie Thornton—'Another great player for Rangers . . . if it wasn't Waddell getting goals at vital times for Rangers then it was Thornton. He was brilliant in the air and could hammer the ball with both feet. Because he built up this reputation in the air people tend, today, to forget just how good his shooting was. I suppose that's understandable when his heading was so good. His timing when he went up for a ball was perfect. And it's timing that counts when you are heading a ball. If you want to get some idea of what I'm talking about then take a look at Alan Gilzean of Spurs. He has the same masterly timing in the air that Willie Thornton had. And I don't think it's any coincidence that Gilzean was signed as a youngster by Willie Thornton at Dundee. He used to work with the young Gilzean at Dens Park and I think some of that old Thornton timing rubbed off on the Spurs' man.'

Inside-left—Alex Venters—'This will probably be a player whose choice will surprise some of the fans—most of the fans, in fact. But Venters was a tremendous team player. He would have made a perfect midfield player in today's game. He has the fitness and the work rate which is demanded from players now.

'He was probably the hardest-working player I ever played alongside. He wasn't big, just stockily built, about the same build as myself, but he made himself go through so much work on the field . . . and not just his own work, either. He pitched in to help anyone who might be in trouble. Again he was a player who worked hard at the game, always trying to improve himself. He had a job near Ibrox and during his lunch hour he would be along at the ground doing extra training all on his own. It was that attitude which would always place Venters in any team of mine.'

Outside-left—Davie Kinnear—'I've kept all the surprises to the end, I suppose, because there will be people who disagree with this choice, too. But Davie is in because of the tremendous first impression he made on me. I played behind him in a Scottish team against England at Goodison. It was the first time I'd played behind him and he was superb. He was fast and he could cross the ball so accurately and he could score goals too. He would have been a better-known player but for the coming of the War. His career was interrupted like so many others and so he didn't get all the recognition that his talents deserved. He could play a bit and, though most people would forget about him in this kind of team, I won't. That game at Goodison means he is always in my team.'

Out of the present day Ibrox squad Shaw names three players who challenge for positions in his all star select . . . the three players who formed the team's backbone last year.

He says: 'I've mentioned Peter McCloy and Derek Johnstone already when I've been discussing Jerry Dawson and Willie

Woodburn. Now, I'd also like to mention Derek Parlane. This is another boy who has worked hard to improve his game and it paid off for him last season. He is fast and strong and a good mover and he must have convinced everyone of his talent when he played for the Scottish League against the English League at Hampden. That night he had to face experienced international players in Roy McFarland of Derby County and Bobby Moore of West Ham and yet he worried them. If he continues to develop as quickly as he has been doing then there's just no saying how good he might become.

'These young players will make their names in the future, though. The men I named for MY team are men I saw playing at the full extent of their talents. I'm judging them as mature men and experienced players. I played with almost all of them for a long time, with some for just a few seasons, with Jim Baxter not at all. But, as a team, I think these are the best candidates for the Ibrox players I have known down through the years. And I think I'd make Woodburn captain of the side because, although he did lose his temper, he had a tremendous

Jock 'Tiger' Shaw holds the first European trophy won by Rangers—the European Cup Winners Cup—in the glittering trophy room. And looking down on him, appropriately enough, is the maker of the modern Rangers, Bill Struth.

feeling for the team and for the game itself. He would make a grand leader and like any good captain he would never be asking any of the other players to do something he would not be willing to do himself.

'He would shout his commands and he would let his presence be felt . . . but then, most of the men I have named, would let the others know they were on the field. That wouldn't be a bad thing . . . after all, it was like that in my days as captain.

'They used to say then that we were always fighting with each other, that we were a "greetin' team". Maybe we were but it was always my feeling that a mistake made on the field should be pointed out when it happened. I didn't see any benefit in telling a player he had made a mistake in the calm of the dressing room when he might have had a chance to think up an excuse. It had to be done right on the spot and if Woodburn or anyone else gave me a taste of my own medicine on the field—and they weren't shy at doing that—then I accepted the bawling out if I had made the mistake. We all accepted it because we were all in the thing together. . . .

'In this team I have picked that same spirit would exist. I only wish I could have sneaked myself into it . . . or even better had the chance to see it play. That would have been something! !'

The Day I Knew I'd Arrived

by DEREK PARLANE

IT WAS just two days before Christmas and Rangers were playing East Fife at Methil. Just an ordinary League fixture. In fact, normally a fixture which is easily forgotten, a fixture which is rarely considered among the glamour clashes of the Scottish First Division.

But last season it was one of the games I remembered most of all—and it will stay that way as long as I live. For that was the day that I knew the Rangers' fans had accepted me as a first team player—and more important, as a replacement for their old idol Colin Stein.

I'd been in the first team for a couple of months, playing away OK, getting a few goals, but still worrying a little bit inside myself about how the fans were taking to me. I had known when I went into the team as the main striker that I had a big, big barrier to beat. You see Colin Stein had been sold to Coventry City and Steiny had been one of the great Ibrox favourites to the fans. Now, here I was, at nineteen taking over his job.

I must say I was worried about it. I knew that I had a big job on my hands and I suppose I lacked a bit of confidence at the beginning because of that. Mind you, the other lads helped me a lot and as time went on I found myself more willing to try things, less apprehensive about passes turning out wrong or shots going wide.

That was the groove I was getting into when we went to Methil on that Saturday, 23 December. Just beginning to settle, to get that little bit cockier, without, I hope, getting big-headed. By 'cockier' I mean confidence in my own ability to do the job I was being asked to do by team boss Jock Wallace.

The one worry left to me was the feeling of the fans. And that day was the day I knew I had arrived. That day was the first day the fans began to chant my name and to a parody of a Christmas carol they belted out from the terracing—'Parlane . . . Parlane

The pose that Derek Parlane learned to hate . . . coach Stan Anderson as he urges on the players in training. But Anderson did so much to shape Parlane's career . . .

. . . born is the king of Ibrox Park'. I felt so great that I could almost have stopped pl ying and turned round to conduct them. I don't know if anyone else will ever know what that meant to me that day.

Suddenly I knew that the fans were behind me, that they were ready to accept me as a successor to Colin Stein and I was delighted. It meant so much to me because I know how discerning the fans at Ibrox can be. They take their time before they make up their minds on any player. Then, once they do, they back them all the way. But, at the same time, I realise that acceptance last season has to be bolstered all the way by top performances. If not then I'll be letting down these same fans who sang for me at Methil and kept right on singing for the rest of the season.

In a way Methil was the beginning for me because it was a break-through to the support . . . but only a couple of months earlier I had wondered just where I would find a place in the team. In any team, for that matter.

You see, at the start of the season I had been caught in a kind of soccer no-man's land. I was a player without a position.

It had happened in a strange way. In fact it's a story which starts back in my school days and then my days with Queens Park as an amateur before joining up at Ibrox. In these days I was a midfield man and nothing else. That was the position I played in from the time I was fourteen but then when I came to Ibrox I was pushed up front in the reserve team and began to score a few goals. I enjoyed it . . . until the affliction that hits every striker at one time or another caught up with me, too. I just stopped scoring goals. The chances that had been so easy suddenly became so difficult. Goals simply dried up and so I was sent back again to the midfield . . . and that move brought me my first real break into the big-time.

John Greig was injured on the eve of the European Cup Winners Cup semi-final second leg against the West German cracks Bayern Munich. I was chosen to play in his place—in midfield, of course—and it was a surprise selection. Most people expected one of the more experienced lads to take over. But on the day of the game I was told that I would be in. Again it was the kind of moment when I couldn't really believe what was happening. Here I was, an unknown, going on to the field against world famous players like Franz Beckenbauer and Gerd Muller and all the others who were to play in the West German team which was to defeat England at Wembley a couple of weeks later.

I know that the reaction of most of the fans when they heard

78   Derek Parlane in his first-ever Old Firm match challenges that
Celtic veteran Billy McNeill for the ball in a heading duel.

that I was in the team that night was 'Derek who?' But I came lucky and scored one of our two goals that night to take us through to the final in Barcelona. Then, against Hibs in the replay of the Scottish Cup semi-final I was badly injured and was out for the rest of the season. When the start of last season came around that's when I was caught out . . . because I knew then that I was not going to make a midfield player no matter how hard I tried, or how long I played.

It was in the early season defeat in the League Cup from Second Division St. Mirren that the fact came home to me. We were beaten 4–1 at Ibrox that night—one of those disastrous early season results—and I had made up my mind that the midfield was no place for me. I felt that I had to play up front if I was going to make it at all.

It was a complete change for me. It was back to square one. Initially when I had been pushed up front in the Ibrox reserves I had felt ill-at-ease . . . now here I was back in my first position and feeling that I had to be a striker. When Colin Stein was sold I got my chance, though, even then I just did not know if things would work out for me.

There was talk of the club buying another centre-forward, talk of Kenny Mackie of Dunfermline and others going to join Rangers and I wondered if that would put me out in the cold once more.

Then in October just before we went to play Motherwell at Fir Park the news came that Mackie didn't want to come to Rangers. I think I knew then that it was up to me. I had to show the club that I could do the job they wanted done. I didn't have to worry about anyone else . . . I simply had to get out there and play my best. It worked out better than I ever dreamed it would.

By the end of the season I had played for the Under-23 team, collected a Scottish League cap against the English League and been in the squad for the Home International series. Yet, if anyone had even suggested that when the season opened I would have said they were crazy.

At that time I didn't even know which position I would be playing in, nor whether I would be in the first team or the reserves again. It's amazing how the whole thing changed.

Yet, as far as I am concerned, I still have a lot of work to do before I'm satisfied that I am doing the job 100 per cent. I still work hard at trying to improve my game. I feel that I can improve my left foot and so I practise at that . . . and I am not happy with my work in the air at cross balls. I feel that I am stronger on one side than on the other and I want to alter that. I'd like to get the work on crosses as good as the work on balls played straight down the middle to me. I work at all of these things . . .

And, after watching Ajax, I am still working at perfecting another part of the game, a part of the game that they showed at its finest.

In the two games we played against them—as part of the Centenary Celebrations—I saw how the experts shield the ball from opposing defenders. They are brilliant at it, the best I've ever seen and I want to be able to do that too.

If there is anyone else I admire for that aspect of the game then it's Martin Chivers, the Spurs and England striker. He does it so well and has the bulk and strength to make it pay off for him. He is probably the striker I admire most of all. When he's on the telly and I'm watching the game I find myself just watching him all the time, whether he is on the ball or not. He has the power and ability in the air and quite simply he looks the part all the time. If I could become as good a player as he is then I'd be happy.

I suppose the two highlights of last season came for me when I played against the English League at Hampden and then helped Rangers win the Scottish Cup on the same ground against Celtic.

The League game was a fantastic experience for me. I had never dreamed that I would be chosen by team manager Willie Ormond. I knew I was being tipped but I didn't think it was on, not after just a few months of first team football. But I was named in the squad and then picked to play. I had to keep pinching myself to believe it as I faced up to Bobby Moore on the park that night. He'd been leading England to their World Cup win when I was still a kid at school and now here I was playing against him . . . it was unbelievable!

It was just as unbelievable to see how calm and controlled he was in everything he did that night. We drew 2–2 and it was a tremendous result for us, especially after the full national team had been hammered 5–0 by England a month earlier. Moore was magnificent. Just the best player I've been up against, always making the game look so simple, always so much in command of every situation. It was an education to play against him . . .

Then not so long afterwards came the second highlight at Hampden . . . the winning of the Scottish Cup. And that was special for me because as well as winning the Cup I was celebrating my twentieth birthday on the same day. I scored one of the goals and I'll never forget that, nor will I ever forget just what the whole thing of winning the Cup meant to all of us at Ibrox. For me it was the climax of the season, a first season that packed everything into six or seven fantastic months.

I established myself in the Rangers' first team. I won a Scottish Cup medal. I played for the Scottish League and then won a full 'cap' in the international against Wales at Wrexham. All in the one season!

It has changed my life a little, of course. From the guy everyone asked 'Derek who?' when I was picked to face Bayern, I'm now known to all the fans.

I can't walk down a street in Glasgow without someone recognising me, talking to me or congratulating me or asking me for my autograph or just pointing at me. I'm asked to supporters' club dinners, to open garden fêtes, to visit children in hospitals and I love every minute of it.

And, in case you wonder, there's just no way I am going to get big-headed about all that has happened to me. There are two reasons for that . . .

At home I have my father, who played as an inside-right for Rangers, as a wing partner to the present general manager Willie Waddell, and he makes sure my feet are firmly on the ground. He has always encouraged me to play the game—but never forced me into it—and when I have had a good game he'll maybe make a grudging comment to that effect. But the only time he really speaks to me about how I've played is when I've done badly . . . then he lets me know all about it. That just makes sure that I don't get carried away.

At Ibrox, then, I have manager Jock Wallace who never allows anyone to get too big for his boots. And I also have the coach Stan Anderson, a person I have to thank for being where I am today. Stan was the man who knocked me into shape in the reserves and in training when I was just at the start of my career with Rangers. He hammered at me all the time. I used to hate him at times because he always seemed to be picking on me.

But now I realise just how much I owe him. He knew what I needed. I'd been at school and then at Queens Park and there you could get away with a casual attitude to the game and to training. At Queens the amateur approach is still the thing and Stan knew he had to knock that out of me. He used to give me extra training, get me back in the afternoons, tell me I wasn't hard enough, ask for more and more effort from me.

81

82   Parlane, in spite of his personal criticism of his ability in the air wins this crucial ball in the Old Firm Final with team-mate Alfie Conn and Celtic defenders Billy McNeill and Jim Brogan looking on.

Seven Celtic players are shown including diving goalkeeper Alastair Hunter as the Parlane header goes for goal. And all stand helplessly.

84   Parlane can be seen again on the extreme left of the picture with goal-maker Alex MacDonald on the extreme right as the ball goes into the net for the equaliser.

Despair for the Celtic players now as Hunter lies beaten on
the ground and the upraised arm of Parlane salutes his own
goal.

The fans go wild in the background and the players celebrate
in front of them. Scorer Parlane is spreadeagled on the ground
as jubilant team-mates congratulate him . . . goal-maker
MacDonald is trying a cartwheel of delight as dejected Celt
Bobby Murdoch looks on.

I felt sometimes I could have hit him because he wouldn't leave me alone. Now, though, I know what he meant. I listened to him and I did what he told me and if I hadn't listened then I wouldn't have had any of the success I have had so far.

I still listen to him and to anyone else who offers me advice and that's something I'd pass on to any youngster like myself. Listen and then work hard and apply yourself. It's the only way. I know it seems hard. I felt that more than anyone, believe me, but I'm happy now that I did work hard. And I'm going to keep on working hard at the game because there is always something new to learn.

Besides, there are so many things I still have to improve . . .

I may have won a medal and a cap in one so-short season. I may have been accepted by the fans and I may have become established in the Rangers' first team. But there's work to be done and I'll be in at Ibrox doing it until I become a better player.

What Rangers Mean to Me

1 Back Home for Bill means IBROX

THERE was a time when Bill Martin left his home in Taransy Street, Govan, and walked along the road to Ibrox where he stood on the terracings and cheered his idols. . . .

Now he still follows them . . . but from slightly further away. From a flat in Baker Street, London, where he now lives and a seat in the directors' box when he travels north to Glasgow, which is just as often as a demanding work schedule allows.

Yet these old beginnings as a Rangers' fan are not too far away from Bill Martin's heart. Because when Martin comes home to Glasgow it means coming home to Ibrox, too. That's really the way this so-successful song-writer looks on his Rangers' allegiance.

For Martin is like any of the other fans who week after week crowd the terracings or cross a continent to watch their team. He dreams the same dreams of glory for Glasgow Rangers, wishes the same nostalgic wishes that, perhaps, he might have been good enough to play for them if only he had done a bit better with that amateur team in Govan.

Now he lives a jet-setting life with offices in London and New York which means regular commuting between these two song-writing capitals.

And when he's in New York and there's a Rangers game being played you can bet his London office will get a call asking for the result. He tells you simply: 'Supporting Rangers doesn't change because your circumstances change or you happen to live in a city away from Glasgow. OK, I'm down here in London now and next week I'll maybe be in New York or somewhere else . . . but I still want to know how the 'Gers are doing.

87

88   Song writer Bill Martin with members of England's 1
World Cup squad, left to right Bobby Moore, Geoff Hurst
Alan Ball, as they launch Bill's song 'Back Home'. But B
one of Rangers' greatest fans. . . .

'It's a way of life, really and it always has been for any Rangers supporter. It doesn't matter that I have moved out of Govan, my roots are still there and some of the roots are at Ibrox.

'I saw them play Moscow Dynamo when I was a kid, just at the end of the war, and I've been addicted ever since. That was in the days when Willie Waddell was on the right wing sending them over for Willie Thornton who was at centre forward—though he didn't play against Dynamo—and now they are still there as general manager and assistant manager.'

We were talking in the plush, and almost cloistered, surroundings of the RAC club in Pall Mall. It's one of the clubs that the thirty-three-year-old song writer uses regularly—though I suspect few of the members would share his unquenchable enthusiasm for Rangers.

Martin has become one of Tin-Pan Alley's most successful song smiths. His biggest successes, 'Congratulations' and 'Puppet on a String' racked up disc scales of more than twelve million, The World Cup ditty he wrote for England's campaign in Mexico—'Back Home'—just failed to reach that magical million mark. Though Bill recalls today—'If they had won we would have had another winner, believe me, I enjoyed doing that song—though I just wished it had been for Scotland.'

'But I liked it anyhow because it involved me in the football business a little bit. I know some of the lads now, like Bobby Moore and Alan Ball and after having a bit of a hit with that one I would like to write a song for Rangers. A good song for their supporters. And I'll do it some time and then sit back when I come to Ibrox and enjoy it all over again when they play it over the loudspeakers.

'Really I started the football song business with 'Back Home' and I would like to do one for Rangers and then hear it at Ibrox.

'I still get a kick out of that sort of thing. Just like I did at Hampden once when I was up for a Scottish Cup Final. Rangers lost that day—beaten 4–0 by Celtic and I was so sick at the end of the game. You know how it is when you lose to Celtic . . . it's just terrible!

'Anyhow there I was feeling awful when suddenly the loudspeakers began to blare out "Congratulations" as Celtic went up to collect the Cup. I just thought to myself, "Well, that's a bit of revenge for the game because the song they were listening to was written by a Rangers' Supporter."

'It· helped a bit—for about a minute I think—and then it was back to gloom.'

90

Though he goes to the directors' box when he gets back to Glasgow—not as often as he would like, but still several times a season—Bill Martin still drops into his old ways. Before the game he can usually be found having a drink with family and friends in a well-known Rangers' howff, The Clachan, in Paisley Road West, a pub not too far from the Stadium.

'I love going in there,' he says, 'because you can soak up all the atmosphere. You feel a part of it all again, listening to all the stories and all the talk about the great games and the great players down through the years. Joining in all the arguments and the rest of it. It's part of being a Rangers' fan—or any football fan, I suppose—getting nostalgic about past glories. You talk about Waddell and Thornton and big Geordie Young, players I remember when I was a kid.

'I was weaned on these names and on their exploits on the field. And then you come more up to date and you remember Jim Baxter and Willie Henderson when they were the kings in the 'sixties and then to today when you have kids coming through like Derek Johnstone.

'That boy Johnstone is something else, isn't he? I saw him in that League Cup Final when we beat Celtic and he scored the goal. Just sixteen years of age and he scores at Hampden to beat Celtic in a final . . . it's unbelievable. And now he's a centre half and he looks as if he could develop into one of the all time greats. After all Willie Waddell has compared him to Willie Woodburn and they don't come much better than that.

'I just get a little unhappy at times, that I don't see them more often. They are only in London every two years or so—and the last time it was terrific. They played Chelsea in a benefit game for the Chelsea captain Ron Harris at Stamford Bridge. That was just perfect for me because when I go to games in London I go to Chelsea because of the show-biz aura that sticks with them. And there they were, my team, Rangers, playing at Stamford Bridge and winning, too, despite all the pre-match suggestions from the London crowd that they would be murdered.

'I loved that night, every minute of it and I had a bonus too, because I took a tenner off Malcolm Roberts in a bet!'

Martin still regrets a little bit that he couldn't graduate much beyond a local amateur team in Glasgow. He wanted to play for Rangers like most kids from Govan did. Now he has altered his ambition. But only a little . . . for he still wants to join the club he has followed all his life. As a director. . . .

He grows very serious when he tells you about his ambition.

It is no gimmick. No publicity stunt . . . just a genuine wish to be connected with the club.

'I've made a bit of money', he says, 'and some time I'll be ready to leave London, get away from the big city bit. When that does happen then I'll be trying to buy Rangers' shares and get on the board. I'd really love that. I'd so like to be connected with the club.

'OK, I never became a player—that was the boyhood dream. 'Now I have the adult dream and maybe I can do something about making this one come right. I know there are problems about becoming a director and living in London, but that could alter. If there's a chance at all then I'll be trying one day to get a seat on the board.

'I love the game and I love the Rangers; to be involved with them officially would be fantastic.

'We will have to wait and see, I suppose, but I'm serious about the whole thing. It's what I would like more than anything else.'

Financially, of course, there would be no problems for Martin whose song successes which began with the Eurovision Song Contest success of 'Puppet on a String' have made him a wealthy man

Anyhow, whether it happens or not it's a dream he cherishes and contingency plans are being formed in his mind to save him embarrassment if ever it does happen.

'You see,' he grins, 'I do have a problem. It's the Rolls-Royce I have just now. I'd have to get rid of it because it's GREEN.

'It was the only colour I could get at the time but I know it would never do at Ibrox. It would have to go, wouldn't it? Then I'd try to get a BLUE one.'

Like the man said . . . it's a way of life! !

2. "Mac the Kilt!"

WHEN Jimmy McMillan flew into the airport at Barcelona before Rangers met Moscow Dynamo in the final of the European Cup Winners Cup he was given a VIP reception by the locals. . . .

Photographs were taken by the Spanish newspapers, autographs were asked for by the airport staff and generally Jimmy, a thirty-four-year-old Glasgow scrap metal merchant and publican, became a pre-match celebrity.

Little wonder! For Jimmy, a small chunky man who is typically Glaswegian, had arrived in the most outrageous of suits . . . an all-tartan outfit loaned to him for the occasion by Glasgow comic Hector Nicoll, a regular performer at the city's Ashfield Club.

'I didn't wear it for a bet, though some of the mates thought I had', laughs Jimmy. 'I wore it because I wanted them to know I was Scottish and that I was there to support my team, the Glasgow Rangers. That was the real reason. I'm proud to be Scottish and proud to support Rangers . . . even though I felt a bit saddened at the end of that game in Barcelona. Still, that's passed now. . . .

'Funny story about it, though. When I got back to Glasgow I returned the suit to Hector Nicoll and a couple of weeks later he stood on the stage at the Ashfield, wearing the suit, and told the audience—'Here it is . . . the only suit banned from Europe for two years!'

'He was referring to that ban on the club . . . it was a bad blow to all of us and especially to the other lads like myself who go with them into Europe.' (*The ban on the club, originally for two years, was later shortened to one year by the European Union—Editor.*)

It was a blow to the fans like Jimmy McMillan who spend so much of their time and their money 'follow following' their team, criss-crossing the Continent the way their fathers used to once travel across Scotland just to see their team. To Jimmy McMillan and these others, a loyal corps, Munich and Amsterdam and Madrid and Copenhagen are almost as familiar to them as Edinburgh and Dundee and Aberdeen.

I've been in sixteen different countries with Rangers and I've never yet failed to see some fans with them . . . even though it might only be friendly games the team is playing. On several of these trips I've bumped into Jimmy McMillan and his mates. He was one of the few fans, for instance, to make the difficult journey to Rennes in the Cup Winners Cup victory year . . . difficult not because of distance but because that Breton town is tucked away from the regular airline routes.

He missed one match that year . . . a date mix-up found him going on holiday with his wife while Rangers were playing in Lisbon.

For the others, though, McMillan was there. And he was travelling again last season to Amsterdam when he appeared in full Highland dress at the second leg of that challenge game against the European Cup holders.

He explains: 'I had worn that kilt at the opening night of the sporting club at Glasgow's Albany Hotel and I liked it. So I just thought that I would wear it again when we went to Amsterdam. It was such a hit that I think I'll be wearing the full rig-out every time I go abroad with the team. It was even better than that tartan suit in Barcelona, believe me.

'Everyone was admiring it. In the city itself, at the Olympic Stadium during the game and then back at the Rangers' hotel. I think that the Rangers' lads appreciated it too. You know how it is, you let people know that you're Scottish and maybe you become a bit of an ambassador.

'I enjoy going abroad with the team. You see great games, exciting games and there is a special atmosphere about these games abroad. They are big football occasions aren't they?

'And I think that you learn a bit about the different peoples you meet in these countries and you get to know other cities. I don't count up what it costs but it's a fair bit of money.

'My wife doesn't mind though, because she used to travel with me at one time. We've no family so I spoil myself a bit by following the team. Often, mind you, you can get to these games on a charter and that means going places a lot cheaper than you could if you went under your own steam. And then there's the fitba' as a bonus.'

Jimmy is mine host at the Misty Inn in Glasgow's Bridgeton area—a pub with a mainly Rangers-biased clientele—and has been supporting the team for fifteen years or more. Over the whole piece he doesn't think that the team which won the Cup Winners Cup was the best he has seen. But he adds quickly: 'In Europe they were the best Rangers team I had watched. That was where they showed their best form. They were magnificent in these matches away from home . . . it was on the Continent that they won that Cup.'

Jimmy McMillan, the man who follows Rangers across 95
Europe pulls a pint for the customers in his Glasgow pub
. . . a Rangers' pub, of course !

Strangely the game he enjoyed most was one that Rangers lost. 'That was the first time I was in Munich with the team', he recalls, 'and we were playing Bayern in the first round of the Fairs Cup. We lost 1–0 but we should have beaten them. John Greig hit the bar, Willie Johnston destroyed them and the whole team was tremendous . . . but we lost. Still it was a great game because it had both teams going forward, both teams trying to win. None of that defensive stuff. Just great football.'

I asked him about Barcelona and the final and the historic victory there. But he was emphatic—'No', he told me, 'no, it can't be that because of the trouble. It was a tragedy for the team that after-the-match business.'

A tragedy, too, for Jimmy McMillan and his like. For the thousands of supporters who don't cause trouble and who spend their lives trekking thousands of miles to see Rangers play.

'I'll be back in Europe with them whenever they're back', Jimmy tells you from behind the bar in his pub. 'You know I've got used to travelling like that with the team. So used to it that I missed it last year. I was glad to get over with them to Amsterdam for the Ajax game . . it kept our hands in so to speak.'

So this season and many others, more countries will be seeing that stocky figure of Jimmy McMillan parading through the streets of their cities, resplendent in his full Highland dress. And few of the people in these cities will have to ask which team he supports. . . .

A Twenty-Seven Years Long Pilgrimage

ANDY BAIN'S long, long pilgrimage with Rangers began in February 1946 on the day he joined the Bridgeton Rangers' Supporters' Club.

And in that twenty seven years it has been interrupted in Scotland just five times. For only five times has the 47 years old Bain missed seeing Rangers play. Laughingly he admits: 'My wife says that I'm not a fanatic but a lunatic about the Rangers. Maybe she's right. All I know is that there is just something in me that is Rangers and always will be.

'I went to Ibrox for twenty four years without missing a game and then one Saturday I was in hospital and I missed a match. That's the only home game I've missed since 1946 and in that time I've missed four away games too. I don't know how much it costs me to travel the country with the team . . . I never think about that. I just know that Rangers are playing and I have to be there. That's the only thing I think about.'

Andy's travels, of course, are not limited to Scotland. He's one of the loyal band of supporters who travel the Continent with the team, too, whenever it is possible.

That started, he says, around fifteen years ago. He recalls: 'It wasn't as common as it is now. European football so far as the British clubs were concerned was still new.

'So it was new to the fans as well. The first time I went with the team was to Holland when they played Sparta Rotterdam. Since that one I've been with them in most places in Europe. I've lost count of the number of places but off hand I'd say I've been to West Germany, Holland, Spain, Portugal, Italy, Sweden, Austria and Belgium. And, of course, I've been to some of the places a few times, now. Like Germany, of course, because the lads have played there so often.

'I've seen all the players at Ibrox since the war, you know since I started going in 1946. Well, when I say I "started going"

97

I mean when I can remember because I was going when I was about eight years old, getting lifted over the turnstiles.

'But, since the war, my top players would be Billy Simpson, Jimmy Millar and John Greig because that's the type of player I like. They were from the same mould, the players who played for the team and who just wouldn't give in.

'Of the present team I'd say Derek Parlane will soon be with that trio. He is looking a great player.

'I think the team is shaping as a really good Rangers' team now. It looks as if our troubles could really be over. . . .'

But whether they are or not Andy Bain will still be at the games, still making the so-rarely interrupted pilgrimage up and down Scotland.

Big George

GEORGE MULHOLLAND is one of that special breed of fans who remain devoted to Rangers—or Celtic—though they live thousands of miles away.

Big George—that's how he is known to the Rangers' players—lives in Toronto where he works as a welder on major construction sites. But, like so many hundreds of others George lives for the weekly news from home . . . the football results on a Saturday. They arrive in Canada around lunch-time on the radio—lunch-time because of the time difference encountered in crossing the Atlantic—and the exiles wait anxiously for the results.

George, though, is sometimes just as liable to pop up at Ibrox to see the game for himself. Over the past three years he has spent thousands of pounds following Rangers. Not from Govan, not from Bridgeton, not from Edinburgh, Dundee or Aberdeen . . . but from Toronto.

He explains: 'I work hard and I make good money but I miss the football and I miss the Rangers. See, sitting around on a Saturday at lunch-time waiting for the results . . . that's murder. We all do it too.

'I suppose getting the results like that is as much of a link with home as anything is.

'But, for me, it's not always enough. I don't have family ties so I can get time off and get home for some of the big games. . . .'

'Time off' is an understatement. In the season Rangers won the Cup Winners Cup, George was home for the full season . . . and squeezed in trips to Lisbon for the Sporting Club match, to Turin for the Torino game and to Barcelona for the Final.

'It was a crazy thing to do,' he admits now, 'but I was sure they were going to win that Cup and I wanted to be there to see it. It would have been terrible to miss that one, the big one.

'I've been lucky in the times I've been over because the players have been good to me with tickets and so on. I met most of them

99

in Toronto when they played there a few years back.'

I was with Rangers then and George Mulholland was one of the supporters who organised life for the players. If they wanted to play golf . . . George fixed it. If they wanted to get gifts for their wives or families . . . George told them where to go. The friendships made then still exist today. . . .

I remember once Nobby Stiles telling me that one sure way to enjoy yourself on a tour in the States or Canada was to stick with Pat Crerand . . . because the Celtic fans would seek him out and make sure he had a good time.

The same applies to Rangers' supporters and to George Mulholland in particular.

He says: 'It meant an awful lot to us just getting the chance to see the team over there. Anything we did was done to make the players feel at home. The supporters there are just as keen as anyone else even though they don't get the chance to see them as often.

'Look at the time I was in Barcelona for the game against Dynamo and I bumped into a few of the Toronto Rangers Supporters Club . . . all over to Spain on a special charter for the game. That's the way these lads are.'

Last season Big George was back for the Scottish Cup Final wearing his Barcelona suit at Hampden and seeing it bring his team luck in another final.

Then it was back home to organise a holiday for Cup Final hero Alfie Conn as a guest of the Toronto Supporters Club and to meet up with his old mate Willie Henderson playing in the States for a team in Miami.

But he will be back this season. 'All I have to know is the European draw and when the games are due and I'll get over,' he promises. 'I suppose it's a long way but I've made the journey seventeen times now and so long as I see the Rangers—especially if they are winning—then I'm happy. The money is well spent. . . .'

Big George is the 'super-fan' among the exiles . . . but he is just one of the fans across the Atlantic who remain Rangers' supporters. He says: 'People talk about a new life . . . but how can you replace the Rangers?'

That sums it up for all of them.

The Clown Prince

WHEN Lex McLean reigned as Glasgow's top comic he did so partly through his acknowledged love for Rangers. . . .

McLean was the Clown Prince of the vast Ibrox support . . . the man who would stand on the stage of the Pavilion Theatre in Glasgow and tell the jokes that would be repeated the following week on the terracings.

And, in a way, McLean reflected the feelings and the humour of the Rangers' fans. There were times when he was unkind . . . but then the fans can be unkind themselves. Mostly, though, McLean was a huge belly-laugh of relief for the supporters and, often, the players, too.

Today at his home in Helensburgh McLean admits: 'I used to play a lot on the Rangers at that time when I was in the Pavilion because I loved the club, I suppose. I went to all the games and so when I was at the theatre on a Saturday night I'd just come out with something about the match that day.

'An awful lot of the Rangers' jokes were ad-libbed and based on something that had happened at the matches. I don't think the players minded.

'There was a spell when George McLean was there that he was often the subject of my jokes but the big fella didn't bother about it. I'd make the same jokes even when he was in the audience.

'The one time I had any trouble was when Dave White was manager and he took exception to some of the cracks I was using in the shows. That passed over, though.

'Basically, I don't think he realised that any jokes I made were made with affection. I love the club and I've been watching them for many, many years.

'It used to be in Glasgow that Tommy Morgan was the top comic and he was a Celtic man . . . so I just let everyone know that I was a Rangers' man and it was successful. Jokes about

101

102   Lex, inside Ibrox, with (left to right) Kai Johansen, Norrie Martin, Willie Mathieson, Billy Semple, Willie Johnston, Alex Willoughby, Davy Provan, Dave Smith, Billy Jardine, Alex Smith, Bobby Watson.

football are part of the Glasgow way of life. There is no getting away from that.'

McLean, after an illness, does not work as extensively as before. But he still goes to the Rangers' games week after week.

He lists among his favourite Ibrox stars down through the years since his days as a Clydebank schoolboy, Bob McPhail, Torry Gillick, Jimmy Smith and Jim Baxter. All, in their own way, were personality players and McLean says: 'I think that Rangers lack some personalities now . . . but I suppose there are fewer around in the whole game. These four players were the type of men I liked. Big Jimmy Smith wasn't the greatest player in the world but what a character he was. . . .'

Maybe Smith's own sense of humour endeared him to Lex. There is a story told of the burly centre-forward playing at Ibrox one day and being constantly admonished by a colleague to 'Do the easy thing, Jimmy, the easy thing.'

After listening to this advice for most of the game the irrepressible Smith eventually lost his temper. He gathered the ball in the clear and then when he heard the advice come as usual, he turned towards the touchline and ballooned the ball high into the stand before turning and asking: 'How's that . . . there was nothing easier to do?'

That's a story that McLean would appreciate . . . and possibly be able to re-tell! !

He tells you: 'The supporters have been good because they have been able to laugh at themselves over the years when nothing has been happening on the field for them. Maybe with the Scottish Cup win all that has changed. I hope so because the support has been starved of success and we need more success now. . . .'

And when Lex talks of his team in THAT way then you know that he is not joking.

Lex McLean cares about Rangers like so many thousands of others. He has laughed at them. He has poked fun at them.

But, all the time, he has followed them and supported them.

A Last Day Title-Decider

RANGERS went about the business of methodically destroying the deadly, dull defensive strategy of East Fife at Ibrox in the closing game of the League season. . . .

But the title they had come so close to was eventually settled elsewhere. In Edinburgh, at Easter Road, where Celtic beat Hibs to notch another title win.

So much credit, though, went to Rangers for the fight they put up, for the way they overhauled and outstripped Hibs who had been so confidently tipped as Celtic's main challengers. And, finally, for the way they made Celtic fight to the very last day of the season to clinch a title they had thought they could win so very much earlier.

Rangers seemed to have tossed their title chances away so early in the season. They had come home from their usual pre-season build-up in Sweden and slumped.

Defeats in the League Cup by St. Mirren and Stenhousemuir were followed by a disastrous opening to the League programme.

At Somerset Park they lost to Ayr United . . . in a High Noon confrontation at Hampden—a midday kick off had been tried to stop crowd trouble—they lost 3–1 to old firm rivals Celtic . . . at Rugby Park they lost 2–1 to Kilmarnock. They did have two victories in this spell at Ibrox, odd goal wins over Partick Thistle and Falkirk which did little to build up either enthusiasm or hope for the future.

Then, in the sixth game, they scrambled a 1–1 draw with Morton at Ibrox and at that stage languishing among the bottom teams in the League with a paltry points total of five from six games.

If any team's interest in the League seemed dead then that team was Rangers. But everyone under-estimated Jock Wallace and his refusal to accept defeat. Everyone under-estimated the players who were soon to show their real form and confound the critics.

This series of five pictures shows the incident which brought Rangers a penalty in the Ibrox League clash with Celtic . . .

Alex MacDonald tries to bring the ball under control as Celtic's Pat McCluskey slides in to tackle. The diving Ranger in the foreground is Alfie Conn.

MacDonald and McCluskey—key figures in the penalty drama—become entangled as Conn falls to the ground and two more Celtic defenders, goalkeeper Evan Williams and right back David Hay come into the picture.

A close-up and it's clear now that McClusky has wrapped his arms around MacDonald's ankles as the Ranger tries to go after the ball and keep his balance . . .

It was a long and hard haul back to a challenging position, but Rangers made the journey and they made it in style. In November they gave a hint of their new-found self-respect when goals from Alfie Conn and and Graham Fyfe gave them a 2–1 win over Hibs at Easter Road.

And, in fact, only in one game, on December 2 at Ibrox did this re-vitalised Rangers' team lose another game. That was against Hearts and it was as big a surprise to the fans who watched as to the thousands who waited expecting to hear that Rangers had won again.

That afternoon they played magnificently. Afterwards Jock Wallace told me: 'We played as well against Hearts as we played against Bayern Munich last season in the semi-final of the Cup Winners Cup.

'Honestly that is how good I thought the lads were and we lost.'

It was a sad day because, truly, Rangers had played well, pushing into all the attacks and then being caught by a sucker punch in the closing minutes of the game. And such a sucker punch it was!

Hearts' inside-forward, little Tommy Murray, was moving down the left with the ball bringing little danger as the Rangers'

108   Alfie Conn raises his arm in appeal as McCluskey lies face down on the ground and MacDonald is hidden behind Williams who has gathered the ball. The other Celt is Jim Brogan.

defence funneled back into position. Then unexpectedly **Murray** stopped in his tracks and cheekily sat down on the ball. **For a** moment the Rangers' players stood perplexed and then **Sandy Jardine** moved in to tackle Murray. That was the moment Rangers lost the game for Murray drew Jardine then chipped the ball over his head down the wing as Jim Brown raced **into** the gap. Brown crossed, Donald Ford rose at the far post and the ball ended in the net. It was too late for Rangers to hit back **and** Murray's piece of gamesmanship lost two points which **might** have helped, in the end, to decide the title.

The fortunate thing for Rangers was that this one slip did not kill their challenge. The new players had brought heart

Referee John Paterson waves away appeals from two Celts,   109
Billy McNeill and Tom Callaghan as he points firmly to the
penalty spot. McClusky remains face down on the turf.

The moment that brought all the tension of an Old Firm game home to young Derek Parlane . . . the moment he almost missed a penalty in the Ibrox League clash which Rangers won 2–1.

Left: Derek Parlane, watched anxiously by this line up of Celtic players moves in to take the penalty.

Right: The young Rangers' striker realises that he has mishit the ball and that goalkeeper Evan Williams has pushed it out and Celtic's Jimmy Johnstone starts to move forward from the line up.

and fire and spirit into the side and one mistake, one bad result, was not going to affect them or kill their hunger for success.

Their next big test was on January 6—against Celtic—at Ibrox and again they rose to the occasion magnificently.

They went in front from the penalty spot—the award made by Referee John Paterson was disputed by the Parkhead players. But, again, the camera shows in the series of pictures that Pat McCluskey did haul down Alex MacDonald.

It was a moment of drama, the kind of drama that invest these Old Firm clashes with a special soccer magic all of their own.

112   As Celtic players move in on him Parlane gets the second
chance he needs as the ball runs towards him.

A man alone—here is Parlane as the Celtic defence begin to chase him as he prepares for his second try.

The ball has gone, Parlane has shot for goal and the ball heads for the net as Jim Brogan makes a despairing attempt to block the try. It's a goal this time . . . but it's a moment the youngster will never forget.

Young Derek Parlane took the kick, mis-hit it against Evan Williams but kept his cool just long enough to follow up and hit the ball into the net.

And then in the second half tragedy when Dave Smith headed a cross from Dixie Deans past his own goalkeeper Peter McCloy and Rangers were up against it. Now, though, the courage of this Rangers' team was shown. In the past this had been enough to make them wilt, enough to make them throw in the towel. This time it simply meant that they had to battle for the winner. It came close to the end of the game when Alfie Conn scored and suddenly the world knew that Rangers' League challenge was for real.

Celtic, under pressure, dropped silly points. Rangers, on the crest, kept building up a formidable list of victories.

They completed a League double over Hibs. They took revenge on Hearts by beating them at Tynecastle. They beat Dundee decisively at Ibrox and they quite simply refused to give up even when a Celtic revival began.

They played in these League games with the same unquenchable spirit, the same relentless running, and the same menacing skill as they showed in winning the Scottish Cup.

This was the Rangers Wallace—and before him Willie Waddell—had been striving to build. It was a team who suddenly brought hope for the future, a team who, at last, seemed to have moved out of the shadow of Celtic, a team who were ready to bring back the success to Ibrox that the fans had been demanding for so long. . . .

The Cup confirmed all that. But it was in the League, on their way to a gallant failure, that the first signs of this new Rangers were seen. It was there that the foundations were built for the Cup victory.

It was there, too, that Rangers showed the consistency which had eluded them down through all the dark and unsuccessful seasons. CONSISTENCY. One word but one which gave meaning to the work that the players had put in on the training grounds and in the games they played.

Rangers' super fitness comes from more than the sand dunes

OVER the past few seasons the whole of Europe has joined in the praise for the super-fit players of Rangers. Foreign journalists and players and coaches have had their say . . . and team boss Jock Wallace was asked to a West German coaching school to talk on how he 'conditions' his players.

At home, too, there has been praise—though, too often, that has been tinged by jokes of Gullane and its now famous sand dunes. It was at Gullane that Wallace began to build his super-fit team with killer runs up the giant dunes.

Runs so severe that players came close to collapse as they battled to finish the course laid out for them. . . .

But it wasn't only in the grim, demanding atmosphere of Gullane that the Rangers' fitness was created. It was also created in the anti-septically clean and quiet atmosphere of the gleaming treatment room at Ibrox.

It is there in that room, surrounded by sparkling, silver machines for the treatment of every injury a footballer can collect, the physiotherapist Tom Craig has his records.

For three years he has painstakingly built up these records on every player at Ibrox . . . and for three years he has worked with Jock Wallace on the training programmes used to make the Ibrox players the fittest in the country.

Craig's so-thorough records are probably the most detailed in the whole of Britain. Not the slightest scrap of information which affects the fitness or possible performance of the players under his charge is missing.

Says the youthful-looking Craig, who helped look after the Scotland team at the last Commonwealth Games in Edinburgh: 'I have spent three years building up these dossiers on the players at Ibrox, and it has involved countless tests on all the players. But, now the job is done and the records of the players in the first team squad are complete. This is something I have always wanted to do. I tried to do it at Clyde when I was physiotherapist there but it wasn't really possible. Clyde were a part-time team and for the kind of tests I wanted to do I needed a lot more time that I could have with the players.

'It's different here at Ibrox. The set-up is totally professional and every facility is there for my work.

'I think that the various tests the players have gone through at regular intervals have been among the most thorough ever done by any football club.

'Obviously my main job is the physical fitness of the players, the actual fitness to play in the team, the freedom from injury, if you like.

'To help me there I have built up records of every injury sustained by every single player. From these we have various break-downs . . . a breakdown to give us the number of knee injuries or ankle injuries or whatever we suffered during the time the records have been kept.

'Then from these details we can work out how many matches have been missed because of players suffering from a specific injury. The other year for instance, we lost a lot of players through fractures. It was a very bad season for us in that way.

'But this year it could be a particular type of ligament injury which bothers us. But by keeping records we know how it can be best treated. You see, we work out the recovery rate for each player who suffered from that injury and then find out the best way to treat it.

'We also have the individual records of each player with detailed notes on their recovery rates. The records also include when they were X-rayed and what for and the results. This means that when a player gets a knock we can very quickly diagnose whether it is a fresh injury, a recurrence of an old injury or, indeed, something that has already been dealt with in another player. We now have a statistical analysis of this kind on all the injuries we have suffered in the last three years.

'Naturally, we don't deal simply in statistics because individual reaction has to be taken into consideration. Some players are simply better at shaking off injuries than others. . . .'

Meanwhile, though, when a player shows certain symptoms, the Ibrox backroom boy can check within minutes through his records for any time that these symptoms have shown up before. Then treatment can be quickly worked out. And it will be the treatment already found to be the best. In the long run what this is going to mean to Rangers is less time wasted on diagnosis because the records are there for guidance; an immediate accurate picture of how long a player may be out of action; this being based on the previous case histories; and, just as important, the previously-tried and trusted treatment being put into operation straight away . . . meaning less matches missed by the injured players.

This must always be the aim of any physiotherapist. He must have his players ready to play again as soon as possible . . . especially if they are important members of the first team squad. Clearly, in cases of severe injury, such as leg breaks, this is not possible. But in the treatment of smaller injuries a return to games sooner than expected by a star player can be of immense value to a team boss.

This is one aspect of Craig's job . . . but for him, it is not nearly the whole picture. For Craig has his other tests . . . tests of heart and lungs and muscle bulk and blood and reaction to training. Tests that are often closely studied by specialists who can learn much from the physical well-being of a highly trained athlete.

Says Craig: 'We realise that there is no physical way to measure skill . . . but there is a basic measure of fitness and we can learn a great deal about the players from the fitness index I have worked out.'

The fitness index is a formula worked out by Craig himself, from the results of all the tests he carries out regularly on his players. And one glance at that fitness index can tell whether a player is shading off or whether a player is holding a peak of fitness.

Clearly a player who drops below his normal fitness index reading is not as good a bet for doing his job on the park as someone who has maintained a top reading.

Says Craig: 'It gives a guide and that is all that it is meant to do. But, at the same time, it can provide a bit of a competitive stimulus to the lads, too. Athletes thrive on a bit of competition and so we post these results every few months and the players know who has gone up or who has slipped back and they react accordingly. You can get someone dropping a little and they are in looking for extra training to boost themselves up the table again.

'Again we have a broad picture of the squad from the fitness index as well as the individual requirements. We are able to pinpoint whether a general training build-up is needed or in individual cases whether extra weight training or track work or whatever is required. I pass all this information on to Jock Wallace and then he decides on the course of action to be taken in the training programme. The great thing is that we can get an immediate feed-back through the index. We can pinpoint pretty accurately what is wrong with a player if his performance is slipping.'

The tests made are intensive. They cover all aspects of the body functions that matter most to athletes. Indeed, not simply to athletes, but specifically to footballers.

Says Craig: 'All the tests must be relative to the playing of football and we realise that.

'Of course something basic to all athletes is heart-lung fitness which is measured by cardio-vascular tests. These determine a player's ability to take in oxygen and use it to its best advantage. We have taken these tests regularly over the three-year spell to assess how each player responds.

'Then there is muscle bulk which is based on height and weight and the spread of muscle, rather than fat over the body. We can increase muscle bulk through weight training and we've had players come to the club, find themselves putting on weight and worrying about it. But this is something that happens when weight is being put on properly . . . when we want a weight increase!

'We have a Vitalograph test which is a lung function test to gauge efficiency of the lungs. Then there is sometimes a bit of psychological testing involved in holding breath and an individual's determination can be gauged on watching him do this too. If two players are doing the test together and one is determined that he won't give in then you'll usually find that he has that same approach on the field of play. It's a guide to his competitiveness.

'Pulse rate is another guide to whether a player is going to fall from a peak of fitness. We take the pulse rate while players are relaxed and after training. Variations tell us how they are reacting. . . .

'Then we have something called a dynamometric grip strength. This is just what it says . . . a test of gripping power. But what it tells us is how a player's reflexes are on either side of his body.

'You find that right footed players show high reaction on that side and vice versa. Now that probably seems natural enough . . . but in goalkeeper you must try to get the reactions the same on either side.

'We found, for instance, that Peter McCloy was weaker on one side than the other. It was very obvious on the test that he favoured one side much more than the other side and Jock Wallace set to work to put that right. He worked on the "weak"

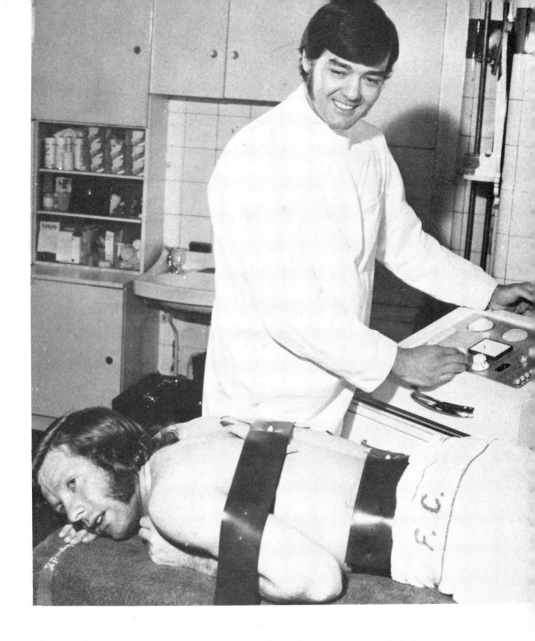

side until now Peter has the same reading for either side. He is as strong on one side as the other, just the way a goalkeeper is meant to be.

'There are other tests, including a heart test, but some are health safeguards mainly, though all of them eventually contribute to the fitness index. By doing the tests regularly we have managed to build up an accurate picture. The tests, usually, were done in July when the players reported back from holiday to

Alex MacDonald is the man seen here getting treatment from
Ibrox physiotherapist Tom Craig in the super-modern treatment room at the Stadium.

start pre-season training, then in August, after the tough training was over, in November, February and at the end of the season in May.'

As well as the May tests that normal closing-down month has the Ibrox players reporting for various inoculations. The inoculations that are so often required when travelling abroad are all done at the same time . . . and all when the players are not playing!

Explains Craig: 'It helps to keep the records if they are done at the same time. And by doing it in the close season it avoids upsets.

'One or two players can be badly affected by vaccinations when they take place. Now, if that is during a season, or just prior to an important European trip, that could mean an under-par performance.'

It is a small detail . . . but important none-the-less and it has been overlooked by clubs before. Many things have been neglected in the past . . . but with Rangers few chances are taken with the fitness of their most important assets. Their players.

Vitamin supplements . . . salt trials . . . Vitamin C surveys . . . all are carried out to make sure that if anything is lost by a player in training then it is replaced immediately.

For instance, when a young player—or an older, experienced player—joins up at Ibrox, Tom Craig hands him a special hand-out on hints on 'Nutrition and Food for Footballers'.

It is a widely informative message and I think by reproducing part of it here I can show the lengths that Ibrox staff go to in their search for fitness for their stars. After a short preamble there is a Guide to Good Eating: this is set out in a table (opposite).

'Remember all meals should contain plenty of protein foods and either fruit or vegetables—cutting down on the carbohydrate foods mentioned in the left-hand column above.'

The hand-out for the players goes on to explain: 'It is natural to expect that individuals such as yourself engaged in strenuous physical activity use more of certain vitamins than the average person, so it is reasonable that besides eating natural foods, extra vitamins should be taken by those training for football. These vitamins should include: The B-Complex Group; Vitamin C and Vitamin E and Wheat Germ oil which contains important endurance promoting factors.

'You may also need to take some form of IRON to help make the red cells of the blood, and thus increase the amount of oxygen which can be carried to the muscles. (Hence the recent blood tests!)'

122

EAT SPARINGLY	EAT THESE FOODS
White sugar and jam. White and ordinary brown bread. Cakes, biscuits and pastry; always avoid foods made mainly with white flower and sugar. Chocolates and confectionery. All soft drinks and artificial flavourings which are fairly concentrated solutions of sugar. Spaghetti and macaroni. Prepared rice and cornflake type breakfast cereals avoiding sugar-coated or chocolate-covered varieties. i.e., rice crispies, coco pops, etc.	Honey, marmite, peanut butter. Whole grain bread, rye bread, and crushed wheat bread. Very nutritious cakes and scones can be made by using whole grain flour, wheat germ and dried fruits. Sultanas and raisins, all dried fruits, peanuts and almonds and other nuts. Milk and pure fruit juices or fresh fruit, e.g., oranges, apples, etc. Meat, fish, poultry, eggs and cheese. Liver and kidneys are excellent and should be eaten as often as possible. Wheat grain porridge if possible or use packed cereals prepared from whole wheat, e.g., Special K, Weetabix. Add one or two spoons of wheat germ (Bemax) and honey for sweetening.

Then follows a number of general hints, stressing that fatty foods should be avoided and that before a game the best food is one that is easily digested and does not lie in the stomach for a long time as fatty foods do.

There is also a warning: 'Use some common sense,' the players are told, 'and do not embark on a "nature-boy" lark. If a natural food—say for example Wheat Germ (Bemax)—disagrees with you, or you dislike it strongly—AVOID IT!'

Then comes another important part of the diet hints . . . the examples of real menus which can be followed by any aspiring soccer star who is reading this.

The examples are as follows: BREAKFAST—Should be leisurely and *not rushed*. Milk or pure fruit juice to drink. Approved cereal with added Bemax, milk and honey or brown sugar. Eggs, poached, boiled or scrambled with grilled bacon or sausages, kidneys, or fish, or cold ham. Tea or coffee is drunk during the meal and wholemeal bread with butter rounds off the meal.

LUNCH—Soup Fresh vegetables. A small quantity is all that is necessary to leave the appetite whetted for the main course.

Main course—Any meat or high protein food. Potatoes served in any manner except fried, salad or other fresh vegetables, e.g., green beans, carrots, cabbage, sprouts, etc. Dessert—Fresh fruit salad with added glucose or honey. Dried fruits (dates, figs, prunes) may be added. No pastries, tarts or ice cream. Cheese or yoghurt may be taken as a substitute. Water should be taken in moderation before lunch and coffee, tea or milk during or after it.

EVENING MEAL—This is the largest meal of the day and is similar in plan to the lunch, the portions generally being heavier. Meat (proteins) as the main course is followed by a dessert and the meal ends with wholemeal bread, butter and cheese. Water can be drunk before the meal and in moderation during the meal if you wish. Tea, coffee or milk is served after it.

'The sample laid out is strictly high protein and may be called your "nutrition for training".

'Obviously what you eat in training must be different from your food requirements as the match day comes near. Your week-day diet contains high, body building proteins. Your match diet should consist of permissible carbohydrates which are easily digested and give a rapid energy output to draw on when required.

'It is not what you eat on the day of the game (that obviously must be light) but what you eat the day before, as the food will be digested and ready to be used efficiently and rapidly when it is most required.'

Every player has this given to him at Ibrox . . . they are advised and encouraged to follow the principles laid down . . . and again, it is just a small part of the whole business of keeping Rangers the fittest team in the country.

There is more thought given to fitness at Ibrox than simply organising a bus run to Gullane. Tom Craig plays his part in the backroom set-up just as the others do . . . and his files give the fitness breakdown that helps the team so much.

124

They want to play for Rangers

WHEN Rangers' Manager Jock Wallace signed four new players towards the end of last season he summed up his moves by telling pressmen—'These boys want to play for Rangers . . . that's what all of them have in common.'

It was a statement that might have obscured other reasons for the signings . . . but one which spelled out the loyalty that Wallace demands from his players. One player had been signed earlier than the others, goalkeeper Stewart Kennedy from Stenhousemuir. He had impressed the Rangers' boss in a League Cup game against the Second Division side at Ibrox early in the season and a careful watch had been kept on his progress. Said Wallace: 'We saw what we wanted and we acted quietly and quickly. . . .'

It was to be the same as the season ended when Rangers shocked Scottish soccer by stepping in to buy Dundee's skipper Doug Houston for £35,000. It was clearly a move to bolster even further the powerful pool of players being built at Ibrox . . . but no one had expected the thirty years old Dundee skipper to be available.

But let Houston tell the story. He told me just after he joined up at Ibrox: 'A year earlier Dundee United had tried to buy me after Jim McLean, the coach at Dens Park, had moved to Tannadice as manager.

'Dundee wouldn't let me go then and so I'd more or less made my mind up that I would be playing out the rest of my career at Dens.

'I had made up my mind to that even though there were times when it got me down a bit. We had been on the verge of having a really good side two or three times and then someone would be sold. I'd seen Jim Steele go to Southampton and then Iain Phillip go to Crystal Palace inside a year and I was beginning to feel that I was in a rut as far as my football was concerned.

125

126   The happy Houstons ready to go . . . Doug, wife Anne and children Kirk and Leigh, ready for the move to Ibrox.

That's when Rangers came along. I was surprised that they had come and surprised again when the transfer was allowed to go through. . . .'

Presumably Dundee allowed their skipper to move because thirty five thousand pounds was a lot of money to receive for a player who is now thirty years old. . . .

But Rangers got the man they wanted and age did not deter them. Nor should it have if you listen to Houston talk about his fitness. He says: 'I don't know how long I'll be able to keep playing but in Dundee you have Doug Smith of United who is still in their side and he is around thirty eight years old. It depends on the individual . . . and I feel one hundred per cent right now.

'I have no weight problems or anything like that and I've been lucky down the years at Dundee that I've had no really serious injuries. There is nothing that can come back to worry me now. Basically I reckon that a player should be at his peak between twenty eight and thirty three . . . so I have a few years left.

'Anyhow, I have a new challenge to spur me, too. At Dens Park my career had come to a standstill. There was nothing left for me. I knew we could finish in the top half-dozen teams in the League and get to a semi-final or two and no one really looked for anything more from you.

'Now it's different. I have to try to make the first team because I was told when I signed that there were no automatic first team places at Ibrox for anyone. So right away I'm out of the relative comfort of Dundee where I knew I would be playing every week and back to fighting for a place in the side.

'And if I get into the team then I know that the prizes are high because at Ibrox people play to win trophies . . . not simply to do well in them. That means I will have the chance of trying to win a European trophy plus the three major tournaments here at home. It's a whole new life and it's what I've always dreamed of.

'When I was a youngster at school I lived in Mosspark and went to Ibrox every week. That was to see the team with Jimmy Millar and Ralph Brand and Davy Wilson and Ian McMillan. I wanted to play for Queens Park and then go to Rangers. As it turned out I did go to Queens and then to Dundee. Now the second part of that dream comes true by joining Rangers . . . and it happened after I had given up all hopes of it ever happening to me.'

Houston knows that there is a fierce challenge for places at Ibrox . . . and so does another new boy Johnny Hamilton from

Hibs. The dark haired Hamilton was one of the surprise free transfer men in Scotland last season. He had made a number of first team appearances for Hibs through the season and his skill and courage were widely respected.

Then suddenly he was released and just as suddenly Jock Wallace swooped. Says Hamilton: 'I could hardly believe it when Rangers said they wanted to sign me. It's what I've always wanted. They are the team I followed as a kid and the team I wanted to come to sign me before I went to Easter Road.

'Now I know it's up to me to take this chance they have given me. I want to play for Rangers more than for any other club in the world. . . .'

For Alastair Scott from Queens Park the message is clear. He follows the last man to leave Hampden for Ibrox . . . Derek Parlane and he sees the success that has come to the young centre-forward. He wants the same and the chance will be given to him.

Says Jock Wallace: 'Just because we won the Scottish Cup and had a good finish to the League championship didn't mean we could sit back and rest on any laurels we might have earned.

'My job is to keep these players working and keep them on their toes. We wanted players and we went after the players and signed them. They have all been told the same thing . . . if you want to get into the first team then earn a place there.

'We don't have room for players who want to be automatic choices . . . we all work together. The players who are in the pool all have the chance to be in the team and that is the only way to run things. Competition for places plus a reserve strength to back us up in any bad time for injuries . . . that's what we have been after. I have tried to get that and I think maybe it's worked out now.

'But, boy, these players are going to work and work again to have them on the boil all the time. We didn't relax after winning the Cup Winners Cup and we won't be relaxing now. We have a job to do and that's all that matters to me. . . .'

The new players found that out early as they slaved under Wallace's demanding instructions at the close-season training sessions.

They will find out even more as they settle into the pattern at Ibrox . . . a pattern designed to bring success.